D1560321

EASY HOMEMADE
BREAD

Brimming with creative inspiration, how-to projects, and useful information to enrich your everyday life, Quarto Knows is a favorite destination for those pursuing their interests and passions. Visit our site and dig deeper with our books into your area of interest: Quarto Creates, Quarto Cooks, Quarto Homes, Quarto Lives, Quarto Drives, Quarto Explores, Quarto Gifts, or Quarto Kids.

© 2022 Quarto Publishing Group USA Inc.
Text © 2022 Ogden Publications

First Published in 2021 by Voyageur Press, an imprint of The Quarto Group,
100 Cummings Center, Suite 265-D, Beverly, MA 01915, USA.
T (978) 282-9590 F (978) 283-2742 QuartoKnows.com

All rights reserved. No part of this book may be reproduced in any form without written permission of the copyright owners. All images in this book have been reproduced with the knowledge and prior consent of the artists concerned, and no responsibility is accepted by producer, publisher, or printer for any infringement of copyright or otherwise, arising from the contents of this publication. Every effort has been made to ensure that credits accurately comply with information supplied. We apologize for any inaccuracies that may have occurred and will resolve inaccurate or missing information in a subsequent reprinting of the book.

Voyageur Press titles are also available at discount for retail, wholesale, promotional, and bulk purchase. For details, contact the Special Sales Manager by email at specialsales@quarto.com or by mail at The Quarto Group, Attn: Special Sales Manager, 100 Cummings Center, Suite 265-D, Beverly, MA 01915, USA.

25 24 23 22 21   1 2 3 4 5

ISBN: 978-0-7603-7351-4

Digital edition published in 2021
eISBN: 978-0-7603-7352-1

Library of Congress Cataloging-in-Publication Data

Bread by Mother earth news : our favorite recipes for artisan
breads, quick breads, buns, rolls, flatbreads, and more / edited
by Karen K. Will.
pages cm
ISBN 978-0-7603-4844-4 (sc)
1. Bread. I. Will, Karen K. II. Mother earth news.
TX769.B77255 2015
641.81'5–dc23
2015011952

Cover and Interior Design: Ashley Prine, Tandem Books
Cover Image: © Anastasiia Kulikovska/Shutterstock
Photo Credits: See page 223

Printed in China

EASY HOMEMADE
BREAD

More Than 150 Recipes for the Beginner Baker

Edited by
Karen K. Will

VOYAGEUR PRESS

Contents

An Introduction to Bread Basics

FLOURS

Bleached vs. Unbleached

When you're shopping for flour, check the packaging. Flour that is labeled "unbleached" has not been chemically treated; it has simply bleached naturally as it has aged. "Bleached" flour, on the other hand, has been chemically treated. Unbleached flour is higher in protein than bleached flour and is best used for yeast breads, pastry, Yorkshire pudding, and popovers. Bleached is best used for quick breads, muffins, pie crusts, cookies, and pancakes.

Choose organic flours when possible to avoid pesticide residues and genetically modified ingredients.

THE BEST OILS AND FATS FOR BAKING

Many recipes for quick breads and muffins call for "vegetable oil," and more often than not, large quantities (1 cup) of it! The evidence now points to the fact that vegetable oils (canola, safflower, corn, soybean, and generic "vegetable") are extremely unhealthy to consume, so we have made efforts to revise our recipes to include healthier alternatives.

Here are a few of our favorite healthy oils and fats that are suitable for cooking and perform well in baked goods:

Virgin coconut oil: It's creamy and buttery with a distinct coconut flavor. An extremely healthy fat, coconut oil is derived from the meat of mature coconuts. Composed mostly of beneficial medium-chain fatty acids, coconut oil resists oxidation and rancidity. It's high in lauric acid, which helps to strengthen the immune system. Coconut oil is solid at temperatures below 70°F. When chilled, it can be used as a substitute for shortening in baked goods. When melted, it can be substituted for any kind of oil called for in recipes.

Melted butter: There is nothing better for taste in baked goods than butter. Butter from grass-fed cows contains more beta-carotene, vitamin A, and conjugated linoleic acid (CLA, a good omega-6 fatty acid) than butter from grain-fed cows. A good substitution for "vegetable oil" in a recipe is half melted butter and half sour cream, e.g., 1 cup vegetable oil = use ½ cup melted butter + ½ cup sour cream.

Lard from pastured hogs: Lard is the original "shortening," and there is nothing better for texture and mouthfeel in baked goods. Lard from pastured hogs is about 40 percent saturated fat, 48 percent monounsaturated, and 12 percent polyunsaturated, making it ideal for cooking. The amount of omega-6 and omega-3 fatty acids varies in lard according to what the pigs have eaten, making fat from pastured or grass-fed hogs the best choice. Lard is also a good source of vitamin D.

Peanut oil: Peanut oil tastes strongly of peanuts, so it's best used when the flavor suits the recipe. It is about 46 percent monounsaturated and 17 percent saturated fat. Avoid hydrogenated oil.

Macadamia nut oil: It's buttery and nutty with a subtle macadamia taste. It has high amounts of oleic acid (a good fatty acid) and anti-inflammatory properties. It's quite expensive, so use it sparingly in recipes or mix with another oil listed here.

Sesame oil: It has a sweet and nutty taste but is not neutral in flavor. Its antioxidants (sesamin) are not destroyed by heat.

Buy organic oils and fats to avoid pesticide residues and genetically modified ingredients.

EQUIPMENT TIPS & TRICKS

Rolled breads can be made with very little specialty equipment. However, certain things can help turn out a superior product and even contribute to a happier, more pleasant baking experience.

Silicone mat: These large nonstick mats are just about perfect for rolling out biscuit or scone dough, pie crust, bread or pizza dough, and for shaping buns and rolls. Though you still have to flour the mat when rolling out dough, it is much less sticky than most surfaces and is easy to clean.

Rolling pins: Endless varieties of rolling pins exist, from silicone to marble and everything in between. We've had good results with French-style (handle less) rolling pins (with nontapered ends) that don't infringe on the diameter of your dough circle.

Marble slabs: These hunks of marble designed especially for dough handling are great if you don't have marble or granite countertops. They keep the dough cold (perfect for biscuit and pie dough) and are somewhat nonstick though require the usual flouring.

Work quickly: With most rolled doughs, but especially with biscuits and scones, it's best to work quickly and ABT—always be turning. Roll a few passes, gently lift and rotate the dough on the work surface, flouring again if needed until the dough is its correct thickness.

HOW TO KNEAD DOUGH

Delicious, yeasty bread is the result of gluten development. Kneading dough is one way to develop gluten that helps to uniformly distribute the gases produced by the yeast. The distribution of gases creates a porous and spongy loaf—the ultimate goal with yeast bread.

Kneading bread is a hands-on undertaking, so don't forget to remove your jewelry and roll up your sleeves before you start.

1. Prepare a work surface. Clean the surface with warm, soapy water, rinse, and wipe dry with a towel. Sprinkle flour over your work surface and spread it around with your hands.

2. In a large bowl, combine the ingredients for your dough. Mix the ingredients well with a wooden spoon. If flour is still sticking to the sides of your mixing bowl, keep stirring until everything is combined. Once all the flour is mixed in and it's difficult to move the utensil through the dough, it's ready to be kneaded.

3. Turn the dough onto your prepared work surface. It should form a loose, sticky ball.

4. Gather the dough into a pile. Sprinkle a little flour over the top and roll it around on the floured board, forming it into a ball. Press down and reshape the dough ball a few times until it is no longer sticky. If the dough doesn't seem to be losing its stickiness, sprinkle more flour over the top and onto the work surface, and work it into the dough.

5. Press the heel of your hand into the dough, pushing forward slightly; this motion is called "punching" the dough and helps the gluten start working. Continue doing this until the dough is slightly springy.

6. Knead the dough by folding it in half and rocking forward on the heels of your hands to press it flat. Turn the dough slightly, fold it in half, and rock into it again with the heels of your hands. Repeat for 10 minutes, or as long as the recipe states. Get into the "zone" and knead at a steady pace. Handle each part of the dough quickly and in turn, never letting it rest for too long before handling it again.

7. The texture of the dough will tell you when it's time to stop kneading. When it's tacky and elastic, and shiny and smooth, it's finished. Until then, keep kneading. Here's a quick test: Drop the dough ball onto your work surface. If the ball holds its shape, it's ready. If you kneaded the dough properly, your bread should have a crunchy crust with a soft, chewy interior. If you stopped kneading prematurely, the bread may turn out tough, dense, and a little flat.

2

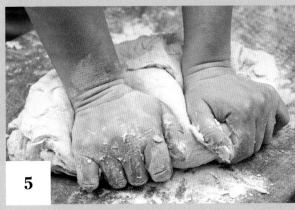

5

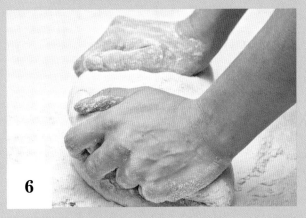

6

3

7

Classic Breads

When it comes to bread making, yeast bread is truly an art form. Why? Because yeast is a living organism and it requires suitable conditions in order to thrive—conditions that you as bread baker must manage. Various combinations of moisture, temperature, oxygen, and food combine to activate yeast and produce alcoholic fermentation, the conversion of sugars into alcohol and carbon dioxide by yeast and bacteria.

There are countless methods for producing a perfectly risen loaf of leavened bread. In this book, we'll provide a sampling of methods and procedures honed from our recipe archives, utilizing different ingredients, equipment, and styles to give you a well-rounded approach to the ten-thousand-year-old tradition of bread baking. From simple white breads to no-knead artisan breads, there is a style of yeast bread to suit your taste and lifestyle.

Read through these recipes well, for they are sprinkled with tips and tricks throughout. Decide how much time, energy, and equipment you have to devote to homemade bread baking. Pick a recipe and roll up your sleeves . . . That yeasty, home-baked aroma is in your near future!

CRUSTY WHITE BREAD

This rustic white bread spreads out as it bakes, which forms natural breaks in its surface crust, creating a dramatic presentation. This bread is made with fairly wet dough, which is a requirement if you want big holes in the crumb, and so it requires only an abbreviated kneading process. It's leavened with a small amount of yeast, which provides the opportunity for a long, cool rise (overnight and most of the next day at a cool room temperature). The long, slow rise lets the yeast and various enzymes develop maximum flavor in the dough, and also makes for a chewy texture. **Yields 1 loaf**

INGREDIENTS

3⅓ cups unbleached all-purpose flour

1 teaspoon active dry yeast
1 teaspoon salt

1⅓ cups water

YOU WILL NEED

Baking stone or baking sheet

Pizza peel or heavy piece of cardboard

Oven-safe pan for water

1. Starting the night before baking day, in a large mixing bowl use your hands or a wooden spoon to mix the flour, yeast, salt, and enough water (start with 1⅓ cups) to form a soft and sticky dough. Cover, and let the dough rise at room temperature.

2. The next morning, wet your hands, lift the dough onto a flat, wet surface, then gently stretch it and fold it in half two to four times. Return dough to the same bowl, cover, and let it rise until it has doubled in size. (If you take the temperature of the dough with an instant-read thermometer and it's below 70°F, you may want to put it in a warm place; otherwise, the rise may take until the afternoon.)

3. While the bread is rising for the second time, line a bowl that will comfortably hold double the amount of dough with a cotton or linen cloth heavily dusted with flour. When the dough has doubled, gently turn out onto a work surface, and with wet hands and a dough scraper (if you have one), stretch and fold, and turn two to four times until the dough begins to stiffen and can be formed into a ball.

4. Place the ball into the bowl on the well-floured cloth. Cover, and let rise until the dough has almost doubled again, 1 to 4 hours depending on room temperature.

5. Place a baking stone or baking sheet in the oven on the middle rack. Place a pan filled with water on the lower rack (humidity in the oven always improves bread crusts). Preheat oven to 500°F.

6. Turn dough onto a well-floured pizza peel or a well-floured piece of heavy cardboard. Slide onto the baking stone or baking sheet in the preheated oven. Bake until the crust is golden brown on top and the bottom crust is hard and thumps like a drum when you tap it (about 30 to 40 minutes). Set to cool bottom-up for at least 2 hours before slicing.

BASIC SANDWICH BREAD

When the meal isn't the bread but what's between the slices, you'll want something light and with a fine crumb. A good sandwich bread recipe produces a loaf that has character but is soft and cake-like and plays the role of supporting actor to the fillings. Historically, American sandwich bread has been lightly enriched with a little fat in the form of milk and oil. This recipe is based on an early eighteenth-century English bread called "French bread." You'll find it has that soft, fine crumb. **Yields 1 loaf**

INGREDIENTS

3½ cups unbleached all-purpose flour

1 tablespoon unsalted butter, softened

1 egg, beaten

1 teaspoon salt

2¼ teaspoons active dry yeast

1¼ cups warm milk

1 egg, beaten and thinned with water, for brushing (optional)

1. In a large bowl, combine the flour with the softened butter. Use your fingers to work the butter into the flour until no large pieces remain. Next, add the beaten egg, salt, and yeast. Holding the bowl with one hand, stir in enough warm milk to form a dough. At this point, the dough should be raggedy and rough.

2. Turn onto a lightly floured work surface. Wash your hands of dough, and with wet hands knead a few times to be sure the dough is well mixed. Place in a clean, lightly buttered bowl and let the dough rise, covered, in a warm place.

3. Butter an 8½ x 4½-inch loaf pan; set aside.

4. After it has doubled in bulk (about 1½ hours), turn onto a lightly floured work surface. Gently press out the gas, form dough into a log, and transfer to the prepared pan. Cover, set in a warm place, and let rise until nearly doubled.

5. Preheat oven to 350°F.

6. When the bread is ready, brush the top of the loaf with the beaten egg thinned with water (optional). Bake until crust is golden, about 1 hour. Remove from the oven, turn out onto a wire rack, and let cool on its side for at least 3 hours before slicing.

OLD-FASHIONED WHITE BREAD

Good, old-fashioned white sandwich bread is a little bit sweet, a lot soft. You know what we're talking about. This is the recipe you've been wanting for grilled-cheese sandwiches and PB&Js. The next time you make tuna or chicken salad, make sure you've made this bread first. **Yields 2 loaves**

INGREDIENTS

⅔ cup sugar

2 cups warm water

1½ tablespoons active dry yeast

1½ teaspoons salt

¼ cup oil or unsalted butter, melted

6 cups unbleached all-purpose flour

1. In a large bowl, dissolve sugar in warm water. Stir in yeast and let sit for 5 minutes.

2. Mix salt and oil into yeast. Add flour, 1 cup at a time, mixing with a wooden spoon. Turn dough onto a lightly floured work surface and knead until smooth. Place dough in a well-oiled bowl and turn over to coat all sides. Cover loosely with oiled plastic wrap. Allow to rise until doubled in size, about 1 hour.

3. Punch down the dough. Turn out and knead for a few minutes, then divide dough in half. Shape into two loaves and place in two well-oiled 9 x 5-inch loaf pans. Let rise for 30 minutes, or until dough has risen 1 inch above the sides of pan.

4. Preheat oven to 350°F.

5. Bake for 30 minutes, until golden brown. Turn out onto a wire rack to cool completely before slicing.

GREEK COUNTRY BREAD

Why do we strive to eat like lords when humble peasant dishes are so tasty? This old-fashioned Greek peasant bread goes well with traditional olives, feta, and stuffed pies.

It's heavy and full of flavor and will be ready by dinnertime if you start right now! The unexpected flavor comes from good-quality honey and olive oil and barley flour. Barley flour is high in fiber and adds a rich nutty flavor to the bread.

This recipe calls for a *brotform*, which is a wicker rising basket that contains the rising/resting dough and prevents sideways spread with wet dough, creating a beautiful pattern of flour that contrasts nicely with slash marks. Brotforms can be found online and at baking-supply stores.

High-gluten flour contains more protein than other flours and is used when an extra chewy (rather than tender) texture is desired. It can be found online at sites such as King Arthur Flour (www.KingArthurFlour.com).

Yields 1 loaf

INGREDIENTS

3 cups high-gluten bread flour

2⅓ cups barley flour

1 tablespoon active dry yeast

2 tablespoons honey

2 tablespoons olive oil

1 teaspoon salt

1½ to 2 cups warm water

1. In a large bowl or stand mixer, combine all ingredients. Mix well. Knead by hand until smooth and elastic, about 10 minutes, or 5 to 8 minutes in a stand mixer. Place in a greased bowl, cover, and let rise in a warm place until almost doubled, about 2 hours.

2. Gently fold to deflate. Shape the dough into a ball and place in a floured brotform. Cover and let rise 1½ to 2 hours, or until doubled.

3. Place a baking stone in the oven and preheat to 425°F. Gently flip the bread out of the brotform and onto a parchment-lined peel or cardboard. Score the round with a sharp knife. Slide the loaf onto the baking stone and bake for 25 to 40 minutes, until the interior temperature reaches 200°F. Remove from oven and let cool for up to an hour before slicing.

4. The bread interior may seem almost undercooked. This is in part due to the barley flour, a low-gluten, high-fiber flour that lends itself to a dense, filling bread.

WHOLE WHEAT BREAD

This half-and-half wheat bread recipe (half whole wheat flour, half white flour) adds flavor and nutrition with whole wheat flour, yet retains some of the lightness of a white loaf; it will be denser than most store-bought wheat breads. If you've got a grain mill and grind your own fresh wheat berries, use this recipe for a nutritious, delicious loaf of bread. **Yields 2 loaves**

INGREDIENTS

2¼ teaspoons active dry yeast

¼ cup warm water

½ cup firmly packed brown sugar

1 tablespoon salt

2½ cups lukewarm water

¼ cup lard or unsalted butter, softened

3½ cups whole wheat flour

4 cups sifted unbleached all-purpose flour, divided

1. In a large mixing bowl, combine the yeast with ¼ cup warm water; set aside.

2. In a separate bowl, dissolve the brown sugar and salt in the 2½ cups of lukewarm water. Add brown sugar mixture to the bowl with yeast, along with the lard or butter, whole wheat flour, and 1 cup of the all-purpose flour. Beat thoroughly to mix well.

3. Stir in the remaining flour to make a dough that leaves the sides of the bowl (forms a ball of dough that sticks together). Turn out onto a floured board, cover, and let rest for 10 to 15 minutes. Knead until smooth and elastic, about 10 minutes.

4. Place dough in a greased bowl and turn over to coat all sides. Cover with plastic wrap or a lint-free cotton or linen tea towel (terry cloth will stick and leave lint on the dough) and let rise in a warm place until doubled, about 1½ hours. (If it is particularly cold in your kitchen or outside, put the dough in the cold oven and put pans of hot water around it. The humidity helps.)

5. Punch down the dough. Turn it onto a floured work surface and divide in half; round up each half to make a ball. Cover and let rest 10 minutes.

6. Shape into loaves and place in two greased 8½ x 4½-inch loaf pans. Let rise until dough peaks 1 inch over the tops of the pans and the top is well rounded; about 1 hour and 15 minutes.

7. Preheat oven to 350°F.

8. Bake for about 45 minutes, covering loosely with foil for the last 20 minutes if necessary, to prevent excessive browning. Cool in the pan for 10 minutes, then turn onto a wire rack to cool completely before slicing.

LIGHT WHEAT SANDWICH BREAD

This soft sandwich bread calls for honey rather than sugar. Honey is not only more healthful, but it imparts a unique, earthy flavor to baked goods that can be altered based on the variety of honey you choose. On average, honey is one to one and a half times sweeter (on a dry-weight basis) than sugar. When using honey in baked goods, you'll notice many differences throughout the process. The batter will be thinner; your baked goods will brown more quickly in the oven (this is normal—just watch carefully and make sure they don't reach the point of no return); and the finished products will be springy and retain freshness longer. **Yields 1 loaf**

INGREDIENTS

1 cup warm water

2¼ teaspoons active dry yeast

¼ cup honey

½ teaspoon salt

2 tablespoons unsalted butter, melted

1 egg

2½ cups unbleached all-purpose flour

1 cup whole wheat flour

1. In a large mixing bowl, combine warm water and yeast. Stir and let stand for about 5 minutes, until frothy. Add honey, salt, butter, and egg; stir well.

2. In a separate bowl, whisk together the flours. Add most of the flour mixture to the yeast mixture and stir until a ball forms. Turn out onto a floured work surface and knead for 5 minutes, gradually adding remaining flour until it's all incorporated. Place dough in an oiled bowl, turning over once to coat. Cover with plastic wrap or a lint-free cotton or linen tea towel (terry cloth will stick and leave lint on the dough) and let rise at room temperature for 2 hours.

3. Turn out dough onto a floured work surface and knead for several minutes. Shape into a log and place in a buttered 9 x 5-inch loaf pan. Press dough lightly but evenly into the pan, making sure it touches all sides. Cover with plastic wrap or a lint-free cotton or linen tea towel and allow to rise again at room temperature for 1 hour.

4. Preheat oven to 400°F.

5. Once the dough has risen and peaks above the pan, bake for 20 minutes. Reduce heat to 350°F and bake for another 17 to 20 minutes, or until internal temperature reaches 195°F when measured with an instant-read thermometer.

6. Turn out onto a wire rack to cool thoroughly (at least 1 hour) before slicing. Store in a plastic bag.

WHITE WHEAT SANDWICH BREAD

If you milk a dairy animal and have an abundance of whey on hand, discover the secret of this flavorful, beautifully textured sandwich bread that is neither too heavy nor too light. The reason that whey improves bread texture is that it's acidic. Commercial bakeries usually use acid in some form (vinegar, citric acid, or even whey) to improve crumb and the shelf life of bread. This versatile recipe can be made into three standard loaves or two dozen rolls, depending on your need. **Yields 3 loaves**

INGREDIENTS

10 cups white wheat flour

2 tablespoons salt

2 tablespoons yeast

¼ cup butter

¼ cup honey

4 cups warm whey plus 1 additional cup of water or whey (If you don't have whey on hand, use half water and half yogurt.)

1 egg

1. In the bowl of a stand mixer fitted with the dough-hook attachment, add the flour, salt, and yeast; mix well. Melt the butter and honey together on low and allow it to cool. Turn on the mixer and, in a slow stream, add the warm whey and melted butter and honey. Allow the mixer to incorporate the ingredients for about 1 minute.

2. At this point there may be a bit of flour on the bottom of the mixer bowl. Stop the mixer and use a rubber spatula to scrape all of the flour and unincorporated dough together. Then turn the mixer on and slowly add as much of the extra liquid to make a soft, slightly sticky dough.

3. Resist the urge to add additional flour. Allow the mixer to knead the dough for at least 5 minutes and no more than 10 minutes.

4. When the dough is smooth and well kneaded, transfer to an oiled bowl and turn to coat all sides. Cover with a plastic wrap or a lint-free cotton or linen tea towel (terry cloth will stick and leave lint on the dough), and set in a warm place to rise, until doubled in size, about 2 hours.

5. After the dough rises, it should lose some of its stickiness. Punch down with well-greased hands.

6. For sandwich loaves, cut the dough into three even portions and form into logs. Place the dough in three 8½ x 4½-inch buttered loaf pans. For rolls, tear off fist-sized portions of dough and form into balls. Place them on a parchment-lined baking sheet. Set in a warm place to rise once again for about 1 hour.

7. Preheat oven to 400°F and place a pan of water on the bottom rack of the oven.

8. In a small bowl, beat the egg with 2 tablespoons of water. Brush the tops of the loaves with the egg mixture and slash each loaf with a sharp knife. Quickly place the loaves in the oven and bake for 45 minutes, until golden brown.

9. Remove the loaves from the oven and turn out onto wire racks to cool. Allow at least 30 minutes to cool before slicing.

OATMEAL SANDWICH BREAD

Oatmeal bread is wholesome, slightly sweet, makes great sandwiches and toast, and is just plain tasty. You can vary the flavor by using cinnamon, or not, and you could use either maple or brown sugar to vary the result. When you want to eat more whole grains like oatmeal to lower cholesterol, reach for this recipe. **Yields 2 loaves**

INGREDIENTS

2¼ to 2½ cups boiling water

1 cup plus 1 tablespoon old-fashioned rolled oats, divided

½ cup maple sugar or firmly packed brown sugar

½ teaspoon maple flavor (optional)

1 tablespoon honey or maple syrup

4 tablespoons butter

1 tablespoon salt

1 teaspoon ground cinnamon (optional)

1 tablespoon instant yeast

1½ cups whole wheat flour

4 cups unbleached all-purpose flour

1 egg, beaten

1. In a large mixing bowl, combine the water, 1 cup oats, maple sugar, maple flavor, honey, butter, salt, and cinnamon, if using. Let cool to lukewarm.

2. Add the yeast and flours, stirring to form a basic dough. Knead dough for about 7 to 8 minutes by hand, or 5 to 7 minutes in a stand mixer with dough hook. Dough should feel smooth and satiny. Transfer to a lightly greased bowl, cover with plastic wrap or a lint-free cotton or linen tea towel (terry cloth will stick and leave lint on the dough), and let rise for 1 hour.

3. Butter two 8½ x 4½-inch loaf pans. Divide the dough in half and shape each half into a loaf. Place the loaves in the prepared pans. Cover with plastic wrap or a lint-free cotton or linen tea towel (terry cloth will stick and leave lint on the dough) and allow the loaves to rise until they peak 1 inch over the edge of the pans. This will take about 1 hour.

4. Preheat oven to 350°F.

5. Brush the tops of loaves with the beaten egg, and sprinkle with remaining 1 tablespoon oats.

6. Bake for 35 to 40 minutes (check for doneness at the 30-minute mark). Remove from oven when golden brown, or when internal temperature reaches 190°F when measured with an instant-read thermometer. Turn out loaves onto a wire rack and cool completely (at least 1 hour) before slicing.

100 PERCENT WHOLE-GRAIN BREAD

Nutritious whole-grain bread doesn't have to be dense and bland. If you've never met a loaf of 100 percent whole-grain bread you liked, try again using this recipe, which produces a surprisingly light loaf rich with flavor.

Here we present the time-tested method of creating pre-doughs, which is discussed at length in Peter Reinhart's *Whole Grain Breads*. Though this method is a little more time consuming than others, the results are worth it. If you're not accustomed to eating 100 percent whole-grain foods, you may want to substitute unbleached bread flour for a portion of the whole wheat flour. Keep in mind that whole wheat flour absorbs more liquid than white flour, so reduce the liquid somewhat if using white flour. You can always add more water later. **Yields 1 loaf**

SPONGE

1¾ cups whole wheat flour

¼ teaspoon instant yeast

¾ cup cool water

SOAKER

1¾ cups whole wheat flour

½ teaspoon salt

½ to ⅔ cup buttermilk or yogurt

2 tablespoons orange juice

FINAL DOUGH

All of Sponge recipe

All of Soaker recipe

1 teaspoon salt

2¼ teaspoons instant yeast

1 tablespoon unsalted butter, softened

2 tablespoons honey

Extra flour and water for adjustments

DAY BEFORE BAKING

1. Make the sponge: Mix ingredients together to form a ball of dough. Knead the dough with wet hands or a stand mixer with the dough-hook attachment for about 2 minutes, then let it rest for 10 minutes. Knead again for about a minute. Cover and refrigerate immediately for at least 6 hours. (This can also be done up to a few days before use.)

2. Make the Soaker: Mix ingredients together to form a loose, wet ball. Cover and leave at room temperature for 6 to 24 hours. (You may also make this a few days before baking, in which case it should be refrigerated.)

DAY OF BAKING

3. Make the loaf: About an hour before you begin mixing your bread, remove the soaker (if it has been refrigerated) and the sponge from the refrigerator to allow them to come to room temperature.

4. Cut or tear the sponge into about a dozen pieces and roll each in the soaker before adding it to the work bowl of a stand mixer fitted first with a paddle, then with a dough hook after the dough comes together. Add the remaining ingredients except the butter and honey. Mix on first speed for 2 minutes, then increase to second speed and mix for another 2 minutes. Add the honey and butter, and mix for another 2 minutes. Let the dough rest in the mixing bowl for 10 minutes.

5. On a floured work surface, knead the dough by hand for a few minutes, adding extra flour and water as necessary to create a soft, slightly sticky dough that is strong enough to resist pulling yet is still malleable. The dough initially feels slack and wet but becomes stronger through resting, kneading, and shaping.

6. Form the dough into a ball and transfer it to a greased bowl, turning the dough to coat it. Cover loosely and let it rise for about 45 minutes. It should be about one and a half times (not double) its original size.

7. Transfer the dough to a floured work surface, form it into a loaf and place it into a greased 9 x 5-inch or 8½ x 4½-inch loaf pan. Cover and allow it to rise for about 45 minutes. Again, it should be about one and a half times (not double) its original size going into the pan. Allowing dough to over-rise weakens its structure, resulting in smaller and misshapen loaves. The dough should be allowed to rise to its fullest extent after it goes into the oven.

8. While the loaf rises, preheat the oven to 450°F. For the best results and the most consistent heat, preheat the oven with a baking stone on the center rack and a cast-iron pan on the top rack.

9. Lightly mist or brush the top of the loaf with water. With a sharp, serrated knife or bread-slashing tool, quickly slash the top of the bread down the middle or make a few diagonal cuts, aiming for a ¼-inch-deep cut. Slashing the loaf gives a place for the dough's gases to escape. If you don't do this, the dough will decide for itself where to puff up.

10. Working quickly, place the loaf pan on the stone in the center of the oven. Immediately add about ½ cup of hot water to the heated cast-iron pan, covering your hand and arm with a kitchen towel to prevent a steam burn.

11. Lower the temperature to 375°F and bake for 20 minutes. (You can spritz the oven walls with a mister early during baking, but be fast and limit your spritzing to only once or twice.) Rotate the pan and bake for another 15 to 20 minutes. For a crisper crust, prop the oven door open slightly with a spoon for the final 5 minutes of baking.

12. The bread is done when the top—including the portion under your slash—is golden brown, the bottom sounds hollow when thumped, and a thermometer inserted into the loaf reads 195°F or above.

13. Remove the loaf from its pan immediately and transfer to a wire rack. Allow the bread to cool at least an hour before slicing.

FARMER'S BREAD

In the Old World, multigrain, whole-grain breads like our farmer's bread were a dietary mainstay for thousands of years. We created this farmer's-bread recipe for a hearty, three-pound loaf from a reference to "opulent farmers" in a 1795 British agricultural text. The farmers ate bread consisting of one part wheat flour, one part rye, and one part barley. This dense, whole-grain bread has sweet undertones from the rye, made more complex by the wheat and barley.

Like all whole-grain breads that are largely based on grains other than wheat, the Farmer's Bread has a sticky crumb until the finished loaf has rested overnight. This powerful bread goes well with strong flavors, such as a richly flavored stew or aged cheddar and chutney. **Yields 1 loaf**

INGREDIENTS

2 cups whole wheat flour

2 cups whole rye flour*

2 cups whole barley flour*

1⅛ teaspoons active dry yeast

2 teaspoons salt

2¾ cups water

YOU WILL NEED

Baking stone or baking sheet

Pizza peel or heavy piece of cardboard

White flour for dusting formed loaf

*Note: Sift out larger grains for a slightly lighter loaf, if desired

1. Starting the night before baking day, in a large bowl, combine the wheat, rye, and barley flours with the yeast, salt, and enough water (start with 2¾ cups) to form a supple yet firm dough. After mixing, work over the dough with wet fists for half a minute or so, until it has a satiny feel. Cover and let rise at room temperature overnight.

2. The bread will not double but will get noticeably softer. In the morning, if you cut into it with a sharp knife, you'll see small air holes. With wet hands, gently punch down the dough, cover, and let rise again for a few hours.

3. Place a baking stone or baking sheet in the oven and preheat to 400°F.

4. Turn the dough onto a lightly floured board and gently shape into an oval or circle. Dust with flour and set aside to rise while the oven heats. Gently lift the bread and place it on a well-floured pizza peel or a well-floured piece of heavy cardboard.

5. Slide onto the preheated baking stone or baking sheet in the preheated oven. Bake for 15 minutes, then lower the temperature to 350°F. After an hour, lower it further to 325°F and bake for another hour. (We like a very strong, crisp crust; unless the bread is burned on the outside or raw on the inside, there is really no right or wrong to baking times. Bake to your taste. If your intuition says that 2 hours is enough, then take it out. If you thump on the bottom of the loaf and the sound is hollow, the bread is done.)

6. When done, remove from the oven and let cool, bottom side up. Do not slice until the next day. You will find that the bread's flavor improves for several days after baking. Store the loaf wrapped in a towel.

BRAIDED ONION BREAD

This savory bread packs an oniony punch and is the perfect companion to your next potluck. Don't be intimidated by this technique; it's not difficult at all if your dough is well prepared. You'll enjoy a great sense of accomplishment and pride when the finished loaf emerges from the oven. **Yields 1 loaf**

DOUGH

2¼ teaspoons active dry yeast

¼ cup warm water

4 cups unbleached all-purpose flour, divided

¼ cup honey

1¼ teaspoons salt

½ cup hot water

½ cup milk

¼ cup unsalted butter, softened

1 egg, beaten

FILLING

½ cup butter

1 cup finely chopped onion

1 tablespoon sesame or poppy seeds

1 tablespoon freshly grated Parmesan cheese

1 teaspoon garlic salt

1 teaspoon paprika

1. In a large mixing bowl or stand mixer, dissolve the yeast in the warm water. Add two cups of the flour—and all the remaining dough ingredients—to the bowl, and blend at low speed (or by hand) for 2 minutes, until everything is well mixed. Stir in enough extra flour—roughly the remaining 2 cups—to form a soft dough. Cover the bowl, set in a warm spot, and allow the dough to rise until it has doubled in size, 45 minutes to an hour.

2. After the first rise is complete, punch down the dough and turn it out on a floured board. Knead until it's no longer sticky, and roll the dough ball out to a 12 x 18-inch rectangle.

3. To make the filling, melt the butter in a saucepan and add the other filling ingredients to the pan and stir. Spread the oniony "sauce" over the rectangular piece of dough, cut the rectangle lengthwise into three 4 x 18-inch strips, and—starting along the 18-inch side—roll up each strip. Pinch the ends closed, place the three 18-inch-long "ropes" buttery seams down on a well-greased baking sheet, and braid them together. Cover with plastic wrap or a lint-free cotton or linen tea towel (terry cloth will stick and leave lint on the dough) and let rise until the dough is light and doubled in size, 45 minutes to an hour.

4. Preheat oven to 350°F.

5. Beat an egg with a little water and brush over the braided dough. Bake for 30 to 35 minutes, or until the braided loaf is golden brown. Let cool in the pan for 10 minutes, then turn out onto a wire rack to cool.

RUSTIC WHEAT BREAD WITH SAVORY HERBS AND ONIONS

This is a wonderful, fragrant loaf of bread to make at the peak of herb season. You can easily substitute whatever fresh herbs you have growing outside your kitchen door to create your favorite flavors—basil, thyme, tarragon. The crunchy, cornmeal crust adds to its savory appeal. **Yields 2 loaves**

INGREDIENTS

½ cup lukewarm water

2 tablespoons active dry yeast

1 tablespoon honey

4 cups unbleached all-purpose flour

4 cups whole wheat flour

2 teaspoons salt

2 cups warm water, divided

4 tablespoons olive oil

¼ cup minced fresh Italian parsley

2 generous tablespoons minced fresh sage

2 generous tablespoons minced fresh rosemary

½ cup finely chopped onion

¼ cup cornmeal, divided

1. In a small bowl, combine lukewarm water, yeast, and honey. Let mixture stand until yeast becomes foamy, about 10 minutes.

2. In a large bowl or stand mixer, combine flours and salt; make a well in the center of the mixture. Add the yeast mixture to the well and stir just to combine a little of the flour. Add 1 cup of the warm water and continue mixing. Add oil and remaining warm water and continue mixing. Once most of the flour is mixed in and it becomes difficult to stir, turn dough out onto a lightly floured surface.

3. Gather dough together and knead for 5 to 10 minutes. Sprinkle with additional flour if sticky, as needed. The dough should be a bit heavy. Place the kneaded dough in a large, lightly oiled bowl to rise, covered with a damp towel. If you are letting the dough rise overnight, cover it with plastic wrap and refrigerate.

4. Once the dough has doubled in bulk, punch it down with your fist, give it a few kneads, turn it over, and either cover it to rise again or prepare to shape loaves.

5. In a small bowl, mix together the herbs and chopped onion.

6. Divide the dough in half and knead each portion, one at a time, gently flattening dough. Spread one-quarter herb mixture on flattened dough and fold it in half to cover, then knead. Flatten dough again and spread another quarter herb mixture on dough, fold over again, and knead. Continue kneading and working herbs and onions into dough, gathering any pieces that fall out. Once dough is homogenous, shape it into a loaf. Repeat process with remaining dough and herb mixture.

7. Lightly sprinkle a baking sheet with half the cornmeal. Place loaves, not touching, on the sheet. Alternatively, you can bake in two buttered 9 x 5-inch loaf pans. Sprinkle tops with remaining cornmeal. With a very sharp knife, make diagonal slashes, ½ inch deep, across tops of loaves. Cover with towel and allow them to rise in a warm place until almost doubled in bulk.

8. Preheat oven to 400°F.

9. Bake for 45 minutes, until golden brown. Cool on a wire rack for 10 minutes before turning out to cool completely.

No-Knead Breads

If you're intimidated by the idea of baking bread at home, the no-knead method is the perfect starting point. If you don't have a lot of time or kitchen equipment, this magical method, which uses just flour, salt, yeast, and water, will introduce you to the world of homemade, thick-crusted, moist-crumbed, *real* artisan bread.

No-knead bread recently came back to life due to professional baker Jim Lahey and his book *My Bread*. According to Lahey, anyone can easily make no-knead, artisan-style bread in a home kitchen with a minimal amount of time, equipment, and effort. It's true!

Making no-knead bread takes a small bit of forethought, some mixing, and a lot of time in between. It's a "slow-rise" method in which the flavor is the result of slow fermentation. The yeast is woken up slowly over time (12 to 18 hours) rather than shocked with warm water and sugar. In fact, this type of bread doesn't call for any added sugar at all. The ingredients are pure and simple—the white loaf calls for flour, salt, yeast, and water only—ingredients that can surely be found in your pantry at this very moment.

You will need a cast-iron dutch oven with a lid. The ideal size is 3½ quarts; any size will work, though the larger the pot, the more the dough will spread out, and the flatter the loaf will turn out. The lid must have a metal knob, or no knob at all; plastic knobs will melt at 475°F. An easy fix for a plastic knob is to replace it with a metal hardware cabinet knob using a screw and some metal washers.

If you find that you love this bread and want to make it repeatedly, invest in some plastic dough scrapers (found online at specialty kitchen stores), which will make dough handling so much easier. Lastly, be aware that a 475°F cast-iron pot is heavy and extremely hot! Use heavy-duty (high-heat) or two sets of pot holders to remove the hot pot from the oven.

Due to the nature of slow fermentation, you'll need to start your bread the day before you want to eat it. This may be hard to get your mind around, but the effort is well worth it. The following method is the most commonly used; you'll find a slight variation to this method in recipes calling for buttermilk, because dairy products burn more easily at higher temperatures.

BASIC NO-KNEAD WHITE BREAD

Yields 1 loaf

INGREDIENTS

3 cups bread flour

1¼ teaspoons salt

¼ teaspoon active dry yeast

1⅓ to 1½ cups cool water

Coarse cornmeal for dusting

1. Combine all dry ingredients in a large mixing bowl. Whisk to combine.

2. Add 1⅓ cups water and stir with a rubber spatula. Add more water, 1 tablespoon at a time, as needed until you have a thoroughly mixed, wet, sticky mass of dough.

3. Cover the bowl with plastic wrap or a lint-free cotton or linen tea towel (terry cloth will stick and leave lint on the dough), and let sit at room temperature, out of direct sunlight, for 12 to 18 hours.

4. After 12 to 18 hours have passed, your dough should be dotted with bubbles and more than doubled in size. (It may also have a strong alcohol smell to it, but never mind that; it will burn off in the baking.) Dust a clean work surface with bread flour and, using plastic dough scrapers or a rubber spatula, scrape the dough loose from the sides of the bowl and turn out onto the work surface in one piece. The dough will be loose and sticky. Dust the top lightly with flour and cover with plastic wrap or a lint-free cotton or linen tea towel. Let the dough rise for another 1 to 2 hours.

5. About 30 minutes before the second rise is complete, place a cast-iron dutch oven without lid on a rack positioned in the lower third of the oven. Preheat oven to 475°F.

6. Once the oven has reached temperature, remove the pot using heavy-duty potholders. Sprinkle about ½ teaspoon of coarse cornmeal evenly over the bottom of the pot.

7. Uncover your dough and, using two plastic dough scrapers, shape the dough into a ball by folding it over onto itself a few times. With the scrapers, lift the dough carefully and let it fall into the preheated pot by slowly separating the scrapers. Dust the top of the dough with a little coarse cornmeal. Cover the pot and bake for 30 minutes.

8. After 30 minutes, remove the lid from the pot and continue baking for an additional 15 minutes, until the loaf is deeply browned.

9. Remove the pot from the oven. With a sturdy wood or metal spatula, nudge the loaf from the pot and transfer to a wire rack. Allow the bread to cool for at least 1 hour before slicing. This cooling time completes the process and is marked by "singing," the popping and crackling sounds the bread makes shortly after being removed from the oven. If you cut open the bread prematurely, you'll end up with a gummy loaf.

NO-KNEAD WHEAT BREAD

Yields 1 loaf

INGREDIENTS

2¼ cups bread flour

¾ cup whole wheat flour

1¼ teaspoons salt

½ teaspoon active dry yeast

1⅓ to 1½ cups cool water

Wheat bran and coarse cornmeal for dusting

Follow instructions for Basic No-Knead White Bread on page 34.

Variation: Dust the bottom of the pot with cornmeal and top of dough with wheat bran before baking.

NO-KNEAD RYE BREAD

Yields 1 loaf

INGREDIENTS

2¼ cups bread flour

¾ cup rye flour, plus extra for dusting

2 tablespoons caraway seeds

1¼ teaspoons salt

½ teaspoon active dry yeast

1⅓ to 1½ cups cool water

1. Follow instructions for Basic No-Knead White Bread on page 34.

2. Dust the bottom of pot and top of dough with rye flour before baking.

NO-KNEAD CRANBERRY-WALNUT BREAD

Yields 1 loaf

INGREDIENTS

3 cups bread flour

¾ cup dried cranberries

½ cup chopped walnuts

1 teaspoon ground cinnamon

1½ teaspoons salt

½ teaspoon active dry yeast

1⅓ to 1½ cups cool water

Coarse cornmeal for dusting

1. Follow instructions for Basic No-Knead White Bread on page 34.

2. Dust the bottom of pot with cornmeal before baking; do not dust the top of the loaf.

NO-KNEAD CARDAMOM-CHERRY BREAD

Yields 1 loaf

INGREDIENTS

3 cups bread flour

¾ cup dried tart cherries

½ cup chopped walnuts

1¾ teaspoons ground cardamom

1¼ teaspoons salt

½ teaspoon active dry yeast

1½ to 1¾ cups cool water

Coarse cornmeal for dusting

1. Follow instructions for Basic No-Knead White Bread on page 34.

2. Dust the bottom of pot with cornmeal before baking; do not dust the top of the loaf.

NO-KNEAD
OAT RAISIN BREAD

Yields 1 loaf

INGREDIENTS

3 cups bread flour

½ cup old-fashioned rolled oats, plus extra for dusting top

½ cup raisins

1 teaspoon ground cinnamon

¼ teaspoon allspice

¼ teaspoon ground nutmeg

1¼ teaspoons salt

½ teaspoon active dry yeast

1½ to 1¾ cups cool water

Coarse cornmeal for dusting pot

1. Follow instructions for Basic No-Knead White Bread on page 34.

2. Dust the bottom of pot with cornmeal and dust top with old-fashioned oats before baking.

NO-KNEAD
SEEDED KAMUT BREAD

Yields 1 loaf

INGREDIENTS

2¼ cups bread flour

¾ cup Kamut flour

1¼ teaspoons salt

½ teaspoon active dry yeast

1 tablespoon ground flax seed meal

½ cup shelled raw, unsalted pumpkin seeds

¼ cup unsalted shelled sunflower seeds plus extra for sprinkling

1 tablespoon sesame seeds plus extra for sprinkling

1 tablespoon poppy seeds plus extra for sprinkling

1½ cups cool water

1 teaspoon honey, mixed into the cool water

Coarse cornmeal, for dusting

1. Follow instructions for Basic No-Knead White Bread on page 34.

2. Dust the bottom of pot with cornmeal and dust top with sunflower, sesame, and poppy seeds before baking.

NO-KNEAD DILL BREAD

Yields 1 loaf

INGREDIENTS

3 cups bread flour

2 tablespoons dried dill weed

1¼ teaspoons salt

½ teaspoon active dry yeast

¾ cup buttermilk or sour milk

¾ to 1 cup cool water

Coarse cornmeal, for dusting

1. These instructions vary slightly from the Basic No-Knead White Bread recipe on page 34; dairy products, like buttermilk, burn more easily at higher temperatures.

2. Combine all dry ingredients in a large mixing bowl. Whisk to combine.

3. Combine buttermilk and ¾ cup water in a measuring cup and add to dry ingredients. Stir with a rubber spatula. Add remaining water, 1 tablespoon at a time, as needed until you have a thoroughly mixed, wet, sticky mass of dough.

4. Cover bowl with plastic wrap or a lint-free cotton or linen tea towel (terry cloth will stick and leave lint on the dough) and let sit at room temperature, out of direct sunlight, for 12 to 18 hours.

5. After 12 to 18 hours have passed, your dough should be dotted with bubbles and more than doubled in size. (It may also have a strong alcohol smell to it, but never mind that; it will burn off in the baking.) Dust a clean work surface with bread flour and, using plastic dough scrapers or a rubber spatula, scrape the dough loose from the sides of the bowl and turn out onto the work surface in one piece. The dough will be loose and sticky. Dust the top lightly with flour and cover with plastic wrap or a clean lint-free cotton or linen tea towel. Let the dough rise for another 1 to 2 hours.

6. About 30 minutes before the second rise is complete, place a cast-iron dutch oven without lid on a rack positioned in the lower third of the oven. Preheat oven to 450°F.

7. Once the oven has reached temperature, remove the pot using heavy-duty potholders. Sprinkle about ½ teaspoon of coarse cornmeal evenly over the bottom of the pot.

8. Uncover your dough and, using two plastic dough scrapers, shape the dough into a ball by folding it over onto itself a few times. With the scrapers, lift the dough carefully and let it fall into the preheated pot by slowly separating the scrapers. Dust the top of the dough with a little coarse cornmeal. Cover the pot and bake for 35 minutes.

9. After 35 minutes, remove lid from pot and continue baking for an additional 10 minutes, or until loaf is deeply browned.

10. Remove the pot from the oven. With a sturdy wood or metal spatula, nudge the loaf from the pot and transfer to a wire rack. Allow the bread to cool for at least 1 hour before slicing. This cooling time completes the process and is marked by "singing," the popping and crackling sounds bread makes shortly after being removed from the oven. If you cut open the bread prematurely, you'll end up with a gummy loaf.

Tip: To make 1 cup of sour milk, place 1 tablespoon vinegar or lemon juice in a measuring cup and add enough milk to equal 1 cup. Stir and let stand for 5 minutes before using.

NO-KNEAD PUMPKIN BREAD

Yields 1 loaf

INGREDIENTS

2½ cups bread flour

½ cup spelt or whole wheat flour

1¼ teaspoons salt

½ teaspoon active dry yeast

1 teaspoon ground cinnamon

½ teaspoon ground nutmeg

¼ teaspoon ground cloves

1 cup puréed pumpkin or butternut squash

¾ cup to 1 cup cool water

2 teaspoons shelled raw, unsalted pumpkin seeds, for dusting

1. These instructions vary slightly from the Basic No-Knead White Bread recipe on page 34.

2. Combine all dry ingredients in a large mixing bowl. Whisk to combine.

3. Combine pumpkin with ¾ cup water in a measuring cup and add to dry ingredients. Stir with a rubber spatula. Add remaining water, 1 tablespoon at a time, as needed until you have a thoroughly mixed, wet, sticky mass of dough.

4. Cover bowl with plastic wrap or a lint-free cotton or linen tea towel (terry cloth will stick and leave lint on the dough) and let sit at room temperature, out of direct sunlight, for 12 to 18 hours.

5. After 12 to 18 hours have passed, your dough should be dotted with bubbles and more than doubled in size. (It may also have a strong alcohol smell to it, but never mind that; it will burn off in the baking.) Dust a clean work surface with bread flour and, using plastic dough scrapers or a rubber spatula, scrape the dough loose from the sides of the bowl and turn out onto the work surface in one piece. The dough will be loose and sticky. Dust the top lightly with flour and cover with a clean lint-free cotton or linen tea towel. Let the dough rise for another 1 to 2 hours.

6. About 30 minutes before the second rise is complete, place a cast-iron dutch oven without lid on a rack positioned in the lower third of the oven. Preheat oven to 450°F.

7. Once the oven has reached temperature, remove the pot using heavy-duty potholders. Sprinkle pumpkin seeds evenly over the bottom of the pot.

8. Uncover your dough and, using two plastic dough scrapers, shape the dough into a ball by folding it over onto itself a few times. With the scrapers, lift the dough carefully and let it fall into the preheated pot by slowly separating the scrapers. Dust the top of the dough with the pumpkin seeds. Cover the pot and bake for 35 minutes.

9. After 35 minutes, remove lid from pot and continue baking for additional 10 minutes, or until loaf is deeply browned.

10. Remove the pot from the oven. With a sturdy wood or metal spatula, nudge the loaf from the pot and transfer to a wire rack. Allow the bread to cool for at least 1 hour before slicing. This cooling time completes the process and is marked by "singing," the popping and crackling sounds bread makes shortly after being removed from the oven. If you cut open the bread prematurely, you'll end up with a gummy loaf.

NO-KNEAD BAGUETTE

. . . .

These baguettes are unlike traditional French baguettes. This version is soft and pillowy inside with a very open crumb, a golden, crispy crust, and the savory addition of olive oil and sea salt on top. They are quite addicting, so don't be surprised when you find yourself ripping off hunks and devouring the bread on sight.

Shaping the loaves can be a little tricky with this wet dough, but perfection is not the goal here—flavor is. You'll want to make this bread over and over, so you'll get plenty of practice with the technique. A baguette pan will produce more uniform results, but a standard baking sheet can be used in its place. **Yields 2 loaves**

INGREDIENTS

3 cups bread flour

½ teaspoon salt

¼ teaspoon active dry yeast

¾ teaspoon sugar

1½ cups cool water

Olive oil, for brushing

Kosher or flaked sea salt, for sprinkling

1. Combine flour, salt, yeast, and sugar in a large mixing bowl. Whisk to combine.

2. Add the water and stir with a wooden spoon or large rubber spatula until you have a thoroughly mixed, wet, sticky mass of dough.

3. Cover the bowl with plastic wrap or a lint-free cotton or linen tea towel (terry cloth will stick and leave lint on the dough) and let sit at room temperature, out of direct sunlight, for 12 to 18 hours.

4. After 12 to 18 hours have passed, your dough should be dotted with bubbles and more than doubled in size. Dust a work surface with flour and, using plastic dough scrapers, scrape the dough loose from the sides of the bowl and turn out the dough in one piece. Using your dough scrapers, fold the dough over and onto itself a few times to form a neat round of dough.

5. Brush the dough with a little olive oil and sprinkle some kosher or sea salt over it, then cover loosely with plastic wrap or a lint-free cotton or linen tea towel. Let the dough rise for another 1 to 2 hours.

6. About 30 minutes before the last rise is complete, preheat oven to 475°F.

7. Once the oven has reached temperature, brush some olive oil on a baking sheet or in the cavities of a baguette pan. Uncover the bread and, using your dough scrapers, cut the dough circle in half.

8. Separate the halves and, using the dough scrapers again as you would your hands, gradually work the dough to elongate each piece to about 12 inches. You may have to fold the ends under or stretch it a little with your hands to create an evenly shaped baguette. Don't overwork it or obsess about getting the perfect shape.

9. Dust your hands with flour and pick up each piece and transfer it to the prepared pan, stretching it a little as you move it. Brush olive oil over the top of each baguette and sprinkle a little more salt. Bake for 15 to 17 minutes, until the bread is golden brown.

10. Remove from the oven and slide onto a wire rack. Allow to cool for at least 1 hour before slicing.

48-HOUR NO-KNEAD CIABATTA

Forty-eight hours seems like a lot of time to devote to bread, but it's akin to those "fix it and forget it" recipes. The hard part is planning ahead two days.

Ciabatta is a relatively new type of bread, first produced in 1982 by Arnaldo Cavallari, a baker from the small town of Adria, near Venice, Italy. Cavallari and other bakers in Italy set out to create a genuine Italian sandwich bread to compete with French baguettes. Ciabatta has become popular throughout Italy, with many regions having their own version, some with a crisp crust and a soft, porous texture; others, like the kind found in Tuscany, Umbria, and Marche, have a firm crust and dense crumb. This recipe is typical for American ciabatta, the more open-crumbed form. **Yields 2 loaves**

STARTER (DAY 1)

1 cup unbleached all-purpose flour

⅛ teaspoon instant yeast

¾ cup water, room temperature

FINAL DOUGH (DAY 2)

2½ cups unbleached all-purpose flour

1¾ teaspoons salt

1 teaspoon sugar

⅛ teaspoon instant yeast

½ cup plus 2 tablespoons water, room temperature

2 tablespoons olive oil

1. Two days (48 hours) before you plan to serve the bread, prepare the starter. In a small mixing bowl, stir together the flour, yeast, and water. Cover and let stand at room temperature for 24 hours.

2. Once 24 hours has passed, prepare the final dough. In a large mixing bowl, whisk together the flour, salt, sugar, and yeast. Add the water, olive oil, and starter and stir with dough whisk or large spoon until dough just comes together into a wet, sticky dough. Cover with plastic wrap or a lint-free cotton or linen tea towel (terry cloth will stick and leave lint on the dough) and let sit 19 hours at room temperature, out of direct sunlight.

3. Using a wooden spoon, stir the dough for a couple of strokes. Cover with plastic wrap or a lint-free cotton or linen tea towel and let it rest for 2 hours.

4. Lightly spray a half-sheet pan or a large baking sheet (18 x 12 x 1 inches) with cooking spray. Line the baking sheet with parchment paper and lightly flour (about 1 teaspoon) in spots where the loaves will go.

5. Turn the dough out onto a floured work surface and sprinkle with lots of flour. Shape the dough into a log and cut in half. Transfer the halves to the prepared baking sheet, with the logs set parallel with the short end of pan. Press the dough into 10 x 4-inch rectangles. Dimple the surface with floured fingertips. Sprinkle each rectangle lightly with flour and cover with plastic wrap or a lint-free cotton or linen tea towel. Let rise for 2 hours.

6. About 20 minutes before the rise is complete, preheat oven to 450°F.

7. Uncover the dough and place in the oven on the center rack. Reduce heat to 425°F, and bake about 30 minutes, or until crust is golden. Remove and let cool on a wire rack for 1 hour.

8. This ciabatta is best the day it's baked, but it can be recrisped in 350°F oven for 10 minutes. Store the bread, wrapped in foil, at room temperature for up to 2 days.

Sourdough Breads

A *sourdough* is defined as "a prospector or settler in the western United States or Canada, especially one living alone: so called because their staple was sourdough bread" (Webster's). Sourdough, the food, is a fermented dough made of wild yeast and a traditional pioneer food of mining camps, chuck wagons, and for those living on the trail. It was known as the best food for energy because of its protein content—according to experts, laboratory tests have shown sourdough contains the greatest amount of protein for its weight and size of any comparable food.

Sourdough was common in pioneer days because yeast was extremely hard to come by, and when it was available, it was almost always "dead" from exposure to extreme conditions. Dead yeast resulted in baking failures, which was a grievous waste of supplies. Sourdough became the standard because it could be controlled and kept alive and was always dependable.

Due to the nature of slow fermentation, you'll need to start your bread the day before you want to eat it. This may be hard to get your mind around, but the effort is well worth it. The following method is the most commonly used; you'll find a slight variation to this method in recipes calling for buttermilk, because dairy products burn more easily at higher temperatures.

Sourdough Starter

The best way to get started with sourdough is to acquire a small quantity of starter from an active pot and then begin feeding it to increase the volume. Ask fellow homesteaders if they'd be willing to give you some of their starter. If not, you can easily make your own. Many complicated starter recipes have been published in books and magazines over the years, but the simplest technique for making starter is to mix together some fresh organic flour with some spring water (avoid chlorinated water, which can kill the microorganisms you're trying to encourage) and set in a warm place for a few days. If you feed it organic, freshly ground flour and good water and keep it at a steady temperature, you'll develop a stable society of microorganisms that will get along quite well.

- You'll need a glass jar or nonmetal mixing bowl to start your culture. Wash it well before you begin, so you don't give any undesirable bacteria a head start. Mix 1 cup organic, unbleached all-purpose flour with ¾ cup water, then cover the bowl lightly with cheesecloth and set it in a place where the temperature will remain warm and constant. Stir the mixture occasionally and check it after 24 to 48 hours. When you see small bubbles beginning to form, start adding equal amounts of flour and water (begin with ¼ cup) once a day for the next 2 days, until the culture becomes very bubbly, possibly even foamy. (If nothing happens, it's probably best to throw the whole mix in the compost bin and begin again.)

- Once the starter becomes active, the microbes will get hungry more quickly. Remove 1 cup of the culture (discard the remainder) and feed it 1 cup of flour and about ¾ cup of water every 12 hours for the next 3 days. By week's end you should have a bubbly, active starter that will become even more lively and flavorful as you use it over the next few weeks.

- You can store your starter in the refrigerator for weeks, even months, between baking. Each time you bake, remember to reserve a cup of the starter and feed it 1 cup of flour and 1 cup of water. Pour this mixture into a wide-mouthed jar or crock, then cover loosely with cheesecloth fastened with a rubber band to permit some air exchange. Allow the mixture to rest for a couple of hours before putting it back in the refrigerator to give the microbes a chance to work on the fresh flour. At some point, a light-brown liquid (called hooch) may form on top. This is a normal development in a healthy culture. Just stir it back into the mixture.

- Make sure to feed it often enough to keep it bubbling and fermenting; but not too often so that you end up with an unusable quantity. If your pot is becoming too full and you won't be using your sourdough for a few days, toss half of it out, and feed it small doses of flour to increase its volume gradually. It's a good idea to stir it every day to aerate, regardless of whether you're feeding it or not. Always stir with a wooden spoon or rubber spatula—never metal, which causes an undesirable chemical reaction.

72-HOUR NO-KNEAD SOURDOUGH BREAD

This is an easy introduction to sourdough bread that you can make if you *don't* have an active starter bubbling on your countertop. Don't let the "72-Hour" bit scare you off; it's really just a few minutes of work and 72 hours of waiting. This bread is best on the day it's baked (and makes great toast), but you can recrisp the crust any time in a 350°F oven for 10 minutes. **Yields 1 loaf**

STARTER (DAY 1)

½ cup unbleached all-purpose flour

⅛ teaspoon instant yeast

¼ cup plus 2 tablespoons water, room temperature

STARTER (DAY 2)

½ cup unbleached all-purpose flour

¼ cup plus 2 tablespoons water, room temperature

FINAL DOUGH (DAY 3)

2½ cups unbleached all-purpose flour

1¾ teaspoons salt
⅛ teaspoon instant yeast

1 cup water, room temperature

1. Beginning three days before you plan to serve the bread, combine the Day 1 starter ingredients in a nonmetallic 1-quart bowl. Cover and let stand at room temperature for 24 hours.

2. After 24 hours, stir in the Day 2 starter ingredients. Cover and let stand at room temperature for 24 hours.

3. Start final dough 24 hours before you plan to serve the bread. In a medium bowl (or 2-quart glass measuring cup so you can easily tell when the dough has doubled), whisk together the flour, salt, and yeast. Add the starter and 1 cup water to the flour and stir with a dough whisk or large spoon until dough just comes together into a wet, sticky dough. Cover with plastic wrap or a lint-free cotton or linen tea towel (terry cloth will stick and leave lint on the dough) and let sit 19 hours in a warm place.

4. Stir down dough (just a couple of strokes), cover with plastic wrap or a lint-free tea towel, and let rest for 3½ hours. About 30 minutes before the last rise is complete, place a cast-iron dutch oven without lid into the oven and preheat to 450°F.

5. When ready, the dough will be more than double in size. Remove the hot pot from the oven and uncover. Place a round sheet of parchment in the bottom to prevent the dough from sticking. Scrape dough into the heated pot. Cover and return to the oven. Reduce temperature to 425°F and bake for 30 minutes.

6. Uncover; bake another 30 minutes, or until crust is beautifully golden and the middle of loaf registers 210°F when measured with an instant-read thermometer.

7. Turn out loaf onto a wire rack and allow to cool for 1½ hours before slicing.

NO-KNEAD SOURDOUGH BREAD

This is a San Francisco–style sourdough loaf, with a crackly crust and a chewy texture. The addition of ¼ teaspoon yeast is up to you. If your sourdough is reliable and always produces perfectly risen breads, there is no need to add it. If not, consider it an insurance policy. **Yields 1 loaf**

INGREDIENTS

3½ cups unbleached all-purpose flour

¼ teaspoon active dry yeast (optional)

1¾ teaspoons salt

⅔ cup sourdough starter (see page 48)

1½ cups water

Coarse cornmeal, for dusting

1. Combine flour, yeast, and salt in a large mixing bowl. Whisk to combine.

2. Combine the sourdough starter and water in a large nonmetallic bowl or mixing cup and add to the flour mixture. Mix with a wooden spoon or rubber spatula until you have a thoroughly mixed, wet, sticky mass of dough.

3. Cover the bowl with plastic wrap or a lint-free cotton or linen tea towel (terry cloth will stick and leave lint on the dough) and let sit at room temperature for 12 to 18 hours.

4. After at least 12 hours have passed, your dough should be dotted with bubbles and more than doubled in size. Dust a clean work surface with bread flour and, using plastic dough scrapers or a rubber spatula, scrape the dough loose from the sides of the bowl and turn out onto the work surface in one piece. The dough will be loose and sticky. Dust the top lightly with flour and cover with plastic wrap or a clean lint-free cotton or linen tea towel. Let the dough rise for another 1 to 2 hours.

5. About 30 minutes before the second rise is complete, place a 3½-quart cast-iron dutch oven (oval-shaped gives best results) on a rack positioned in middle of oven. Preheat oven to 450°F.

6. Once the oven has reached temperature, remove the pot using heavy-duty potholders. Sprinkle about ½ teaspoon of coarse cornmeal evenly over the bottom of the pot.

7. Uncover your dough and, using two plastic dough scrapers, shape the dough into a ball by folding it over onto itself a few times. With the scrapers, lift the dough carefully and let it fall into the preheated pot by slowly separating the scrapers. Dust the top of the dough with a little coarse cornmeal. Cover the pot and bake for 35 minutes.

8. After 35 minutes, remove lid from the pot, rotate, and continue baking for an additional 15 minutes, or until loaf is nicely browned.

9. Remove the pot from the oven. With a sturdy wood or metal spatula, nudge the loaf from the pot and transfer to a wire rack. Allow the bread to cool for at least 1½ hours before slicing. This cooling time completes the process and is marked by "singing," the popping and crackling sounds bread makes shortly after being removed from the oven. If you cut open the bread prematurely, you'll end up with a gummy loaf.

SOURDOUGH SANDWICH BREAD

This bread is soft with a dense crumb, perfect for standing up to sandwich toppings or grilled cheese. If your sourdough is very active and predictable, omit the addition of yeast. Sourdough will keep longer than regular loaves; store this in a plastic bag for up to a week at room temperature. **Yields 1 loaf**

INGREDIENTS

½ cup warm water

1 teaspoon active dry yeast (optional)

½ cup sourdough starter (see page 48)

2 tablespoons sugar

½ teaspoon salt

2 tablespoons unsalted butter, melted

1 egg

3½ cups unbleached all-purpose flour

1. Combine warm water and yeast in a large mixing bowl and stir. Let stand for 5 to 10 minutes, until frothy.

2. Add sourdough starter, sugar, salt, butter, and egg; stir well.

3. Add most of the flour to the bowl and stir until a ball forms. Turn out onto a floured work surface and knead for 5 minutes, gradually adding remaining flour until it's all incorporated.

4. Place dough in an oiled bowl, turning over once to coat. Cover with plastic wrap or a lint-free cotton or linen tea towel (terry cloth will stick and leave lint on the dough) and let rise at room temperature for 2 hours.

5. Turn out dough onto a floured work surface and knead for several minutes. Shape into a log and place into a buttered (or nonstick) 9 x 5-inch loaf pan. Press dough lightly and evenly into pan, making sure it touches all sides. Cover with plastic wrap or a lint-free cotton or linen tea towel and leave to rise again at room temperature for 1 hour.

6. Preheat oven to 400°F.

7. Once dough has risen and peaks above the pan by ½ inch, uncover and bake for 20 minutes. Reduce heat to 350°F and bake for an additional 17 to 20 minutes, until internal temperature reaches 195°F when measured with an instant-read thermometer.

8. Turn out loaf onto a wire rack to cool thoroughly (at least 1 hour) before slicing.

SOURDOUGH BISCUITS

This recipe is easy and fun to make—the biscuits can even be baked in a dutch oven over coals in the great outdoors, pioneer-style. They have that characteristic flaky crust (enhanced when you use lard) and soft, tart insides. **Yields 3 dozen biscuits**

INGREDIENTS

2 cups unbleached all-purpose flour

2 cups sourdough starter (see page 48)

½ teaspoon salt

1 tablespoon honey

2 teaspoons baking powder

2 tablespoons lard or unsalted butter, chilled and cut into small pieces

2 tablespoons butter, melted

1. Preheat oven to 350°F. Grease a 10-inch cast-iron skillet; set aside.

2. In a large bowl, mix together all ingredients, except the melted butter, until a soft dough forms.

3. Pinch off egg-size pieces and roll between palms to form balls. Place dough balls, touching, around the edge of the skillet in concentric circles until filled. Brush tops with melted butter. Set the skillet in a warm spot for 10 minutes to allow biscuits to rise.

4. Bake for 35 to 40 minutes, until golden brown. Serve immediately with butter and honey.

SOURDOUGH OATMEAL BREAD

This bread is perhaps the perfect food—healthy oats and sourdough in combination. Oats are loaded with fiber, heart-healthy antioxidants, and B vitamins, and when fermented in a high-protein sourdough bread, offer substantial health benefits like blood-sugar stabilization. Health benefits aside, this loaf is delicious to boot. **Yields 2 loaves**

INGREDIENTS

2 cups sourdough starter (see page 48)

3 cups unbleached all-purpose flour

1½ cups rolled oats (either old-fashioned or quick)

2 tablespoons olive oil

1½ teaspoons salt

3 tablespoons honey

1 to 1¼ cups lukewarm milk

1. Combine all ingredients in a large bowl or the bowl of a stand mixer. Mix until a soft, loose dough forms. Cover and let sit for 30 minutes.

2. Lightly dust a clean work surface with flour. Turn out the dough and knead for 5 to 10 minutes, until dough is smooth. The dough will still be quite wet, which is OK if you are using a stand mixer. If you are kneading by hand, you may need to add a little more flour to keep the dough from sticking. Just add as little as possible so the dough stays soft and loose.

3. Place the dough in an oiled bowl, cover, and let rise in a warm place for about 2 hours. Sourdough mixtures don't rise as high as traditional breads. This mixture will puff up, but you probably won't see a doubling of the dough.

4. Grease two 9 x 5-inch loaf pans.

5. Divide the dough in half and shape into two loaves. Transfer dough to the prepared pans and cover with plastic wrap or a lint-free cotton or linen tea towel (terry cloth will stick and leave lint on the dough). Set in a warm place to rise for 1 to 1½ hours.

6. Preheat oven to 375°F.

7. Bake for 50 to 55 minutes, until the internal temperature reaches 200°F when measured with an instant-read thermometer.

8. Turn out loaves onto a wire rack and allow to cool for at least 30 minutes before slicing.

SOURDOUGH HAMBURGER BUNS

If you've got a bubbling sourdough starter on your countertop, this is the recipe for you. You can add lots of delicious goodies to your hamburger bun recipes, but remember that the burger, tomato, lettuce, mayo, and mustard are the star players, and the bun is there in a supporting role. With that in mind, adding a tablespoon of minced chipotle, jalapeño, or red pepper flakes; a teaspoon of cracked black pepper; or some Parmesan, Romano, or sharp cheddar can add zing to your buns.

Or go crazy and add oat flakes and other grains or onion bits for a really rustic bun. Note that small seeds such as caraway, fennel, poppy, and sesame can be mixed dry with the dough or sprinkled on top, but hard seeds may need to be boiled in water for one to two hours, then squeezed well to remove excess moisture before they are added to the dough. **Yields 8 buns**

INGREDIENTS

2 cups sourdough starter (see page 48)

3 tablespoons unsalted butter, melted

½ cup milk

2 eggs, beaten

1 teaspoon salt

2 tablespoons sugar

3 cups unbleached all-purpose flour

1. Pour the sourdough into a large nonmetallic mixing bowl. In a separate bowl, combine the butter, milk, eggs, salt, and sugar; beat with a fork to mix, then add to the sourdough. Mix in the flour 1 cup at a time until the dough is too stiff to mix by hand.

2. Turn the dough out onto a floured work surface and knead in the remaining flour until the dough is smooth and satiny. Roll the dough out to ½ inch thick and cut with a 4-inch round cutter. Place the buns on a greased baking sheet at room temperature until doubled in bulk.

3. Preheat oven to 350°F. Bake the buns for 15 to 18 minutes, until golden brown. Cool on a wire rack.

SPELT SOURDOUGH BUNS

These tasty buns are perfect for hamburger buns or dinner rolls. Plan ahead because you need to start them the night before. Spelt flour, an ancient grain, imparts an earthy nuttiness in these rolls—they are dense without being too heavy. Sourdough bread likes to take its own sweet time, but the flavor is well worth it. **Yields 8 buns**

INGREDIENTS

1 cup sourdough starter (see page 48)

½ cup water

½ cup milk

1 egg

2 tablespoons olive oil

2 teaspoons salt

3½ cups whole spelt flour

1. In a nonmetallic bowl, combine the starter with the water, milk, egg, olive oil, and salt. Stir in the flour. The goal is to have a loose dough, so you should still be able to move the dough around with a spoon. Cover the bowl loosely with plastic wrap or a lint-free cotton or linen tea towel (terry cloth will stick and leave lint on the dough) and set in a warm place to rise overnight for at least 12 hours.

2. The next day, turn the dough out onto a well-floured work surface and knead until pliable, adding more flour if needed. The dough should come together quickly. Let it rest for 20 minutes, then divide the dough into 8 equal portions. Form rounds out of each piece of dough, place on a well-oiled baking sheet, and flatten gently. Loosely cover with plastic wrap or a lint-free cotton or linen tea towel. Let it rise in a warm place until the rolls have doubled in size. This may take 2 to 4 hours.

3. Preheat oven to 425°F. Bake the rolls on the top rack of the oven for 20 to 30 minutes, until puffed and golden brown.

SOURDOUGH BLUEBERRY MUFFINS

These muffins are a delightful cross between a biscuit and a muffin, with a unique texture and bright flavor, thanks to the lemon zest. The recipe calls for dried blueberries like the sourdoughs would have used in their day, and the dried berries impart a pleasing chewiness. You can soak the blueberries in hot water for a few minutes to soften, but it's not absolutely necessary; fresh blueberries can be substituted. **Yields 12 muffins**

INGREDIENTS

- 1 cup sourdough starter (see page 48)
- 1 egg
- 4 tablespoons unsalted butter, melted and cooled
- ½ cup sugar
- 1 teaspoon lemon zest
- 2 cups all-purpose flour
- ½ teaspoon baking soda
- 1 teaspoon baking powder
- 1 cup dried blueberries

1. Preheat oven to 400°F. Grease a standard muffin pan or line with paper cups; set aside.

2. In a large nonmetallic bowl, mix together the sourdough starter, egg, melted butter, sugar, and lemon zest.

3. In a separate bowl, sift together the flour, baking soda, and baking powder and fold into sourdough mixture just until moistened. Do not beat or overmix.

4. Dust blueberries with a little additional flour and gently fold into batter. Divide batter evenly into the muffin pan.

5. Bake for 25 minutes, until golden brown. Cool on a wire rack for 5 minutes before turning out. Serve with butter and blueberry preserves.

SOURDOUGH HOT CROSS BUNS

This particular recipe is not your usual hot cross bun recipe—it's even better. Most recipes call for plenty of warm spices like cinnamon, cardamom, and nutmeg. For this version, though, we use ground mace. Mace is made from the lacy covering of the nutmeg and has a less pronounced, but just as unique, flavor.

Instead of the usual purchased candied fruit peel, we call for candied Meyer lemon peel. (Candied orange peel would be good here, too.) We use currants, which are as sweet as raisins, with just a touch of tartness. Unlike raisins, currants really come into their own once they are cooked. And to top off these delicious sourdough rolls, the icing is made with orange juice instead of milk, for an added boost of flavor.

These rolls are best served the same day as they are baked but can also be frozen (before they're iced) and served at a later date. Keep the dough as soft as possible, and don't overknead it. **Yields 12 buns**

INGREDIENTS

2 cups sourdough starter (see page 48)

¾ cup milk

1 egg

5 tablespoons unsalted butter, melted

3½ to 4 cups unbleached all-purpose flour

¼ cup firmly packed brown sugar

½ teaspoon salt

1 teaspoon ground cinnamon

¼ teaspoon ground cloves

¼ teaspoon ground allspice

¼ teaspoon ground mace

⅓ cup currants

⅓ cup chopped, candied Meyer lemon peel

1 egg plus 1 tablespoon water, beaten together, for egg wash

GLAZE

½ cup powdered sugar

1 tablespoon orange juice

1. In a large bowl or stand mixer bowl, combine the sourdough starter, milk, egg, and melted butter until well mixed. Add the flour, brown sugar, salt, and spices, and knead until dough is combined. Add currants and candied lemon peel. Knead until dough has a satiny sheen; 8 to 10 minutes by hand, or 5 minutes in a stand mixer.

2. Divide dough into 12 pieces. Roll each into a ball and place on a greased or parchment-lined baking sheet. Cover and let the buns rise in a warm place for 2 to 3 hours.

3. Preheat oven to 400°F. Brush the top of each bun with the egg wash. Snip the top of each bun with kitchen scissors (in the shape of a cross), if desired.

4. Bake for 20 to 30 minutes, until browned.

5. Remove buns from baking sheet and cool on a wire rack. When the buns are completely cool, combine the glaze ingredients and drizzle over the buns, forming a cross.

Buns & Rolls

· ·

Buns and rolls are an art unto themselves. So many factors influence the finished product, from the room temperature and humidity to the stickiness of your work surface; trial and error comes into play when turning out these baked goods. However, as long as you keep that in mind, they are certainly fun and easy enough to make. Plus, making a few of these special recipes will give you admirable experience with dough handling!

From homemade hamburger buns to iced cinnamon rolls, the recipes here range from everyday use to holiday treats. Some require that you start them the day before baking; others can be whipped up in an afternoon. The perfect roll or bun may be something of a legend, but don't let that discourage you from honing your craft. There is no substitute for homemade baked rolls and buns hot out of the oven—they will delight and surprise your guests.

24-HOUR HAMBURGER OR HOT DOG BUNS

After you discover the rich goodness and simple ingredients of homemade hamburger buns, you'll never be satisfied with store-bought buns again. But can you bake your own hamburger buns without a special hamburger-bun pan? Of course you can! Place the dough balls on a baking sheet about 2 to 3 inches apart, as directed in this recipe. After a 10-minute rest, press them down with the palm of your hand—not flat, but somewhat spread out. Do it again 10 minutes later if they aren't about 4 inches across. They should be about right after the final rise.
Yields 8 buns

INGREDIENTS

2½ cups unbleached all-purpose flour

2 tablespoons sugar

2¼ teaspoons instant yeast

1 teaspoon salt

¾ cup water

1 egg, lightly beaten

2 tablespoons olive oil or butter, melted

1. In a large bowl, whisk together the flour, sugar, yeast, and salt. With dough whisk or wooden spoon, stir in water, egg, and oil until blended. The dough will be very sticky. Cover with a lid, plastic wrap, or lint-free tea towel (terry cloth will stick and leave lint on the dough) and place in the refrigerator for at least 24 hours, or up to 3 days.

2. On the day the buns will be served, remove dough from refrigerator. On a lightly floured work surface, knead the dough gently for 1 to 2 minutes.

3. For hamburger buns, divide the dough into 8 equal pieces, about 3 ounces each; use a kitchen scale to get the weight right. Roll each into a smooth ball. Place on a greased baking sheet and flatten gently into 3½-inch disks.

4. For hot dog buns, divide dough into 8 equal pieces. Roll each into a 5-inch-long cylinder. Place on a greased baking sheet and flatten slightly.

5. Cover and let rise until doubled, about 1 hour. During the last 15 to 20 minutes (depending on your oven), preheat oven to 400°F.

6. Bake for 20 minutes, until golden brown. Remove buns from the baking sheet and place on a wire rack to cool. Slit buns before serving.

WHOLE-GRAIN HAMBURGER BUNS

Homemade hamburger buns taste fresher and better than anything you can find at the grocery store, and if you choose to make them with healthy whole grains, you'll have a leg up on nutrition, too. **Yields 6 buns**

SPONGE

1 cup warm milk (If you need to proof your yeast, reduce the milk to ¾ cup, and proof yeast in ¼ cup warm water.)

4 tablespoons unsalted butter, partially melted in the warmed milk

¾ cup whole wheat flour

1 cup unbleached all-purpose flour

¼ teaspoon instant yeast

2 tablespoons potato flour (or instant potato flakes)*

¼ cup King Arthur's Baker's Special Dry Milk*

3 teaspoons King Arthur's Whole Grain Bread Improver*

*These additives are optional, but yield lighter, more flavorful buns. If you don't use them, add an extra ¼ to ½ cup all-purpose flour.

DOUGH

¼ cup warm water

2 teaspoons instant yeast

1¼ cups unbleached all-purpose flour

2 tablespoons sugar

1½ teaspoons salt

TOPPINGS (OPTIONAL)

1 egg white beaten with 1 tablespoon water

Sesame seeds, oat flakes, or other seeds and grains

1. The night before baking, in a large bowl, mix together the sponge ingredients, cover with plastic wrap or a lint-free cotton or linen tea towel, and allow to rest at room temperature overnight, or for at least 2 hours. In a separate bowl, pour a little water over any hard seeds or grains that you plan to use as topping, and let them soak overnight. Softer seeds can be added dry.

2. In the morning, make the dough: Mix the yeast into the warm water, and work that mixture into the sponge. Then mix in the remaining dough ingredients. Knead the dough (in a stand mixer or by hand) until it is smooth and elastic (about 10 minutes in a mixer). If the dough is unmanageably sticky, add a few more tablespoons of flour. If it's too dry, add a little water.

3. Place the dough in a lightly greased bowl, turning to coat all sides. Cover the bowl with plastic wrap and a lint-free cotton or linen tea towel.

Let the dough rise in a warm spot for about an hour, until it has doubled in bulk. If you plan to add a seed topping on your buns, put an egg on the counter and let it come to room temperature before separating the white.

4. Turn the dough out onto a lightly floured surface and divide it into 6 pieces. Roll each piece into a smooth ball and place it on a baking sheet. Cover the pan with plastic wrap or a lint-free towel and let the buns rest for about 10 minutes. Then remove the towel only and press down on the tops. Replace the towel and let rise until puffy, about an hour.

5. Preheat oven to 375°F. Just before baking, remove the plastic wrap and towel and brush each bun top with the egg white/water mixture, and sprinkle with desired topping.

6. Bake buns for 15 to 20 minutes, until golden brown. Remove from the oven and cool on a wire rack.

CARAWAY-RYE HAMBURGER BUNS

For this recipe, which makes extremely light and delicious buns, we worked with the baking experts at King Arthur Flour. They answered our queries patiently and provided some real insight into the bun-making process. For example, a sponge works with whole grains, because it fires up the yeast and softens the wheat bran, making it easier for gluten strands to develop.

Why use King Arthur's Baker's Special Dry Milk instead of standard dry milk? They say that dry milk from the store is freeze-dried and contains an enzyme that interferes with gluten development. But King Arthur's heat-drying process inactivates that enzyme, so the gluten strands develop more fully, and the buns rise until light and airy. **Yields 6 buns**

SPONGE

1 cup warm milk (If you need to proof your yeast, reduce the milk to ¾ cup and proof yeast in ¼ cup warm water.)

4 tablespoons unsalted butter, partially melted in the warmed milk

¾ cup rye flour

1 cup unbleached all-purpose flour

1 tablespoon caraway seeds

¼ teaspoon instant yeast

2 tablespoons potato flour (or instant potato flakes)*

¼ cup King Arthur's Baker's Special Dry Milk*

3 tablespoons King Arthur's Rye Bread Improver*

*These additives are optional but yield lighter, more flavorful buns. If you don't use them, add an extra ¼ to ½ cup all-purpose flour.

DOUGH

¼ cup warm water

2 teaspoons instant yeast

1¼ cups unbleached all-purpose flour

2 tablespoons sugar

1½ teaspoons salt

TOPPINGS (OPTIONAL)

1 egg white beaten with 1 tablespoon water

Sesame seeds, oat flakes, or other whole/milled seeds and grains of your choice

1. The night before baking, in a large bowl, mix together the sponge ingredients, cover with plastic wrap or a lint-free cotton or linen tea towel (terry cloth will stick and leave lint on the dough), and allow to rest at room temperature overnight, or for at least 2 hours. In a separate bowl, pour a little water over any hard seeds or grains that you plan to use as topping, and let them soak overnight. Softer seeds can be added dry.

2. In the morning, make the dough: Mix the yeast into the warm water, and work that mixture into the sponge. Then mix in the remaining dough ingredients. Knead the dough (in a stand mixer or by hand) until it is smooth and elastic (about 10 minutes in a mixer). If the dough is unmanageably sticky, add a few more tablespoons of flour. If it's too dry, add a little water.

3. Place the dough in a lightly greased bowl, turning to coat all sides. Cover with plastic wrap or a lint-free cotton or linen tea towel. Let the dough rise in a warm spot for about an hour, until it has doubled in bulk. If you plan to add a seed topping on your buns, put an egg on the counter and let it come to room temperature before separating the white.

4. Turn the dough out onto a lightly floured surface and divide it into 6 pieces. Roll each piece into a smooth ball and place it on a lightly greased baking sheet. Cover the pan with plastic wrap and a lint-free cotton or linen tea towel and let the buns rest for about 10 minutes. Then remove the towel only and press down on the tops. Replace the towel and let rise until puffy, about an hour.

5. Preheat oven to 375°F. Just before baking, remove the plastic wrap and towel and brush each bun top with the egg white/water mixture, and sprinkle with desired topping.

6. Bake buns for 15 to 20 minutes, until golden brown. Remove from the oven and cool on a wire rack.

HOT CROSS BUNS

An Easter tradition in historically Christian countries, hot cross buns are sweet, yeast-leavened rolls made with spices and dried fruit. The cross piped across the top with icing (or small strips of dough) is a symbol of the crucifixion. For a different take on this classic, substitute dried cranberries or cherries (or a combination) for the raisins or currants. Serve hot cross buns with butter and cheese. Note to bakers: Don't add more than the 1 teaspoon cinnamon, or the dough won't rise well. **Yields 9 buns**

INGREDIENTS

3 cups bread flour

¼ cup sugar

½ teaspoon salt

1 teaspoon ground cinnamon

1 tablespoon active dry yeast

½ cup milk

3 tablespoons unsalted butter

1 egg

⅓ cup currants or raisins (optional)

½ cup chopped mixed candied fruit (optional)

1 beaten egg white for glaze, if desired

ICING

½ cup powdered sugar

1 to 2 teaspoons milk

1. In a large bowl, mix the flour, sugar, salt, cinnamon, and yeast.

2. Pour the milk and butter into a small bowl and warm in the microwave to about 120°F as measured with an instant-read thermometer. Stir into the dough.

3. Add the egg, currants, and candied fruit, if using. Make a soft dough, adjusting for more or less milk or flour, depending on the dough's consistency. Turn dough out onto a lightly floured work surface and knead gently for about 10 minutes.

4. Transfer to a greased bowl, turning to coat all sides. Cover with plastic wrap or a lint-free cotton or linen tea towel (terry cloth will stick and leave lint on the dough) and let rise in a warm place for about 1 hour.

5. After the first rise, punch down and divide into 9 balls, and place them into a greased 9 x 9-inch baking pan. Cover with the tea towel again, until doubled, about 30 to 45 minutes. If you want the buns to be shiny, brush with beaten egg white.

6. Preheat oven to 350°F. Bake the buns for about 40 minutes, until golden brown. Cool on a wire rack.

7. When the buns are cool, mix together the powdered sugar and milk in a small bowl until a smooth paste forms. Drizzle or spoon the traditional *X* across the top of each bun.

EVERLASTING ROLLS

These basic, yeasted rolls are made with potatoes—beloved for the soft and fluffy texture they impart, and the slightly sweet-and-sour flavor. They're "everlasting" because you can keep the dough in the refrigerator for up to one week. Bake them all at once for a crowd, or pinch off just what you need and serve them all week with supper.
Yields about 3 dozen rolls

INGREDIENTS

3 cups lukewarm water, divided

2¼ teaspoons active dry yeast

1 cup lukewarm mashed potatoes

1 cup lard or unsalted butter, melted

1 cup sugar

1 tablespoon salt

1 teaspoon baking powder

6 to 8 cups unbleached all-purpose flour, divided

2 tablespoons butter, melted, for brushing

1. In a glass measuring cup, combine 1 cup of the lukewarm water with the yeast; stir and set aside.

2. In a large bowl, combine potatoes, lard or unsalted butter, sugar, salt, baking powder, remaining 2 cups lukewarm water, and 3 cups of the flour; mix well. Mix in the dissolved yeast. Let stand in a warm place for 30 minutes.

3. Work in enough of the remaining flour so the dough can be handled and kneaded. The more you knead the dough, the finer and nicer the texture of the rolls. Cover and set in a warm place for about 2 hours, then punch down and let rise again.

4. Form dough into rolls, any shape you desire, and place on two ungreased baking sheets. Let rise again, about 15 minutes. Put baking sheets into a cold oven and turn temperature to 400°F. Bake for about 25 minutes, until golden. Remove from the oven and brush tops with the melted butter.

DINNER ROLLS FOR A CROWD

This recipe makes dinner rolls for an army, like when you are having twenty-six guests for Turkey Day. If you are the least bit squeamish about large-batch baking, feel free to halve the recipe. We've added some dry milk to this recipe for tenderness; you can use King Arthur's Baker's Special Dry Milk, available from King Arthur Flour, or ordinary dry milk. **Yields about 4 dozen rolls**

INGREDIENTS

2 teaspoons sugar

½ cup lukewarm water

1½ tablespoons active dry yeast

3 cups hot water

½ cup lard or unsalted butter

1 tablespoon salt

1 tablespoon sugar

8 to 9 cups unbleached all-purpose flour

2 to 3 tablespoons nonfat dry milk powder

3 tablespoons butter, melted, for brushing

1. In a glass measuring cup, dissolve the sugar in the lukewarm water, then add the yeast and let stand for 10 minutes, until foamy.

2. In a large bowl, combine the hot water, lard or butter, salt, and sugar. Stir to melt the shortening and cool while the yeast is proofing. Stir in the yeast mixture. Add flour, 2 cups at a time, and stir well. Add the dry milk powder and stir until stiff. Let the dough rest for 10 minutes.

3. Turn the dough onto a floured work surface and knead, adding more flour as needed to prevent sticking, about 8 to 10 minutes. Place the dough in a greased bowl, turn to coat, cover, and let rise for 1 to 1½ hours until doubled in size. Punch down the dough, shape into rolls, and place in greased muffin pans. Cover and let rise for 30 minutes, again, until doubled.

4. Preheat oven to 350°F. Bake rolls for 15 minutes, until golden brown. Remove from pans to a wire rack, and brush with melted butter.

CRESCENT ROLLS

The Midwest's favorite staple food, the crescent roll, doesn't have to pop out of a cardboard tube nor contain harmful ingredients we can't pronounce. Have fun with the kids re-creating this beloved roll, but you might want to double this recipe if your family loves these as much as we do.

Crescent dough has a different texture than regular yeasted dough. It is lighter and softer and needs to be treated delicately. **Yields about 24 rolls**

INGREDIENTS

2 cups warm water

⅔ cup nonfat dry milk powder

2 tablespoons active dry yeast

¼ cup sugar

2 teaspoons salt

½ cup unsalted butter, softened

1 egg

4½ to 5 cups unbleached all-purpose flour, divided

1. In a large bowl, dissolve the dry milk powder in the water. Add the yeast and stir slightly; let rest for a few minutes. Add the sugar, salt, butter, egg, and 2 cups of the flour; mix slowly. Slowly add 2 more cups of the flour and start stirring it more swiftly. Add another ½ cup of the flour and mix until smooth. Transfer the dough to a clean, oiled bowl (so the dough does not stick) and cover the bowl with plastic wrap or a lint-free cotton or linen tea towel (terry cloth will stick and leave lint on the dough).

2. Set dough in a warm spot and allow to rise for 45 to 60 minutes. Line a baking sheet with parchment paper and set aside.

3. When the dough has doubled in size, turn it out onto a lightly floured work surface and divide in half. Roll each half into a circle. Cut each circle into 8 (or 16 if you want smaller rolls) even wedges. Roll each piece into a crescent starting at the wide (outside) edge and rolling toward the center (point). Place each roll on the prepared baking sheet. Set aside to rise again.

4. Preheat oven to 375°F. Bake rolls for 15 to 20 minutes, until golden. Cool on a wire rack.

QUICK AND EASY SPOON ROLLS

These delicious treats are basically yeast rolls disguised as muffins. They're easy to make, with no fancy shaping or fussing required. **Yields 24 rolls**

INGREDIENTS

3¾ cups unbleached all-purpose flour

¼ cup sugar

2¼ teaspoons instant yeast

1¼ teaspoons salt

2 cups water

½ cup unsalted butter

1 egg, lightly beaten

1. In a large bowl, whisk together the flour, sugar, yeast, and salt. In a saucepan or in the microwave, heat the water and butter together until butter is melted and mixture is 120–130°F when measured with an instant-read thermometer. With a dough whisk or large wooden spoon, stir the liquid into the flour mixture along with the egg until blended. The dough will be very sticky. Cover and let rise until doubled, about 35 to 45 minutes.

2. Grease two standard muffin pans or line with paper cups; set aside. Stir down the dough with just a few strokes. Scoop dough into muffin pans using a ¼ cup measuring cup, filling two-thirds full (scant ¼ cup). Let rise, uncovered, for 20 to 30 minutes, until dough has risen to the tops of the cups. During the last 15 minutes of rising, preheat oven to 400°F.

3. Bake for 20 minutes, until rolls are golden brown. Let stand 5 minutes before removing from pans.

CRUSTY WATER ROLLS

These are called "water rolls" because, like water crackers, they are neutral in flavor and can accompany almost any dish. The hot water placed in the oven provides moisture that gives these rolls the perfect texture. If you desire, glaze unbaked rolls with a beaten egg white and/or sprinkle seeds such as poppy or sesame on top. **Yields 18 rolls**

INGREDIENTS

1 cup warm water

1 tablespoon sugar

2¼ teaspoons active dry yeast

1½ teaspoons salt

3½ to 4 cups unbleached all-purpose flour, divided

2 tablespoons olive oil

2 egg whites

Fine cornmeal, for dipping

1 egg yolk, beaten with 1 tablespoon water

1. In a large bowl, combine the warm water, sugar, and yeast. Let stand until bubbly. Add salt, 1 cup of the flour, and oil; beat until smooth.

2. With an electric mixer on high speed, beat egg whites until stiff. Fold into batter.

3. Beat in 2 more cups flour, making a stiff dough. Turn dough out onto a floured work surface; knead until smooth. Add flour as needed to prevent sticking.

4. Place dough in a greased bowl and turn to coat all sides. Cover with plastic wrap or a lint-free cotton or linen tea towel (terry cloth will stick and leave lint on the dough) and let rise until doubled. Punch down, cover, let rise 15 minutes more.

5. Pour a little cornmeal into a bowl. Grease a baking sheet. Punch down the dough and divide into 18 pieces. Shape each piece into a ball; dip the bottom in cornmeal and place on the prepared baking sheet, about 2 inches apart. Cover and let rise until doubled in size.

6. Preheat oven to 400°F. Place a pan of hot water on the bottom rack of the oven. Brush rolls with egg-yolk mixture. Bake rolls on a rack above the hot water for 15 to 20 minutes, until golden brown. Cool completely on a wire rack.

WHOLE WHEAT HONEY ROLLS

These sweet whole wheat rolls are not only delicious and soft but they're a healthier version of the dinner roll. These are perfect for those fall-harvest dinners when folks want food that'll stick to the bones. **Yields about 5 dozen rolls**

INGREDIENTS

1 cup butter

½ cup honey

2 cups boiling water

4½ teaspoons active dry yeast

⅓ cup warm water

2 eggs, beaten

1 teaspoon salt

1 teaspoon baking powder

3½ cups whole wheat flour

3½ cups unbleached all-purpose flour

¼ cup butter, melted, for brushing

1. Place butter and honey in a large bowl; pour boiling water over both and set aside. In a glass measuring cup, combine yeast and warm water; set aside to dissolve.

2. When honey mixture has cooled, stir in yeast mixture, eggs, salt, and baking powder. Stir in whole wheat flour and enough all-purpose flour to make a soft dough. Turn onto a lightly floured work surface, and knead until smooth, 8 to 10 minutes.

3. Place dough in a greased bowl, turning to grease the top. Cover with a damp cloth and set aside to rise until doubled in size, about 1 hour.

4. Punch down the dough; let rest 10 minutes. Grease a baking sheet. Shape into dinner rolls and place on the prepared baking sheet.

5. Preheat oven to 375°F. Cover rolls and let rise until doubled in size, about 20 minutes. Brush the tops with melted butter.

6. Bake for 15 to 20 minutes, until rolls are lightly browned and sound hollow when tapped. For a softer crust, brush with melted butter after baking and cover with a cloth to cool.

QUICK BUTTERMILK ROLLS

These are quick and easy because after a quick knead of the dough, you simply pinch off 12 equal pieces and place them in a greased muffin pan to rise and bake. **Yields 12 rolls**

INGREDIENTS

2¼ teaspoons active dry yeast

½ cup warm water

1 cup lukewarm buttermilk or sour milk (see page 40)

3 tablespoons lard or unsalted butter, softened

1 teaspoon salt

¼ teaspoon baking soda

1 teaspoon sugar

2½ to 3 cups unbleached all-purpose flour

1 tablespoon butter, melted, for brushing

1. In a large bowl, combine yeast and warm water. Let stand 5 minutes. Add buttermilk, lard or butter, salt, baking soda, and sugar; mix well. Stir in 2 cups of the flour, 1 cup at a time. Add remaining flour and mix to make a soft dough.

2. Turn the dough out onto a floured work surface; knead 5 minutes, or until smooth. Divide the dough into 12 equal parts; shape into rounds, and place in a greased muffin pan. Cover and let rise until double, about 1 to 2 hours.

3. Partway through the rising time, preheat oven to 400°F. Bake rolls for 15 to 20 minutes, until golden brown. Transfer to a wire rack to cool, and brush crusts lightly with melted butter, if desired.

ICEBOX ROLLS

These old-fashioned "icebox" rolls got their name because the dough can be stored in the refrigerator for up to two weeks. We love these for the holidays, when we can either bake them all at once for a big dinner or just use what we need and bake for the family. This recipe comes in quite handy. **Yields about 3 dozen rolls**

INGREDIENTS

2¼ teaspoons active dry yeast

¼ cup lukewarm water

1 cup milk

⅔ cup lard or butter

⅔ cup sugar

2 teaspoons salt

1 cup mashed potatoes

2 eggs, beaten

6 to 6½ cups unbleached all-purpose flour

1. In a glass measuring cup or small bowl, dissolve yeast in warm water; set aside.

2. In a small saucepan, bring milk to scalding; transfer mixture to a large bowl. Add lard or butter, sugar, salt, and potatoes. Cool to lukewarm. Add yeast mixture and eggs.

3. Stir in flour, 1 cup at a time, to form a soft dough. Turn dough out onto a lightly floured work surface and knead until smooth. Place dough in a greased bowl; cover and let rise about 2 hours. Punch down dough, then cover tightly and place in the refrigerator until ready to use. The dough can be stored up to 2 weeks.

4. About 2 hours before serving, remove dough from the refrigerator. Form dough into rolls, and place on a greased baking sheet. Let rise until doubled in size, about 1½ hours.

5. Preheat oven to 375°F. Bake for 20 to 25 minutes, until golden. Serve immediately.

PECAN CARAMEL ROLLS

Let's not pretend that this dish will help "start your day right." However, pecan caramel rolls are a special treat and loved by many, so they can be served as a dessert or brunch item on occasion, and no one will be worse for wear. The gooey pecan topping is irresistible yet easy to make, and the clean-up is well worth the trouble.
Yields 12 rolls

INGREDIENTS

1 cup milk

¾ cup granulated sugar, divided

¼ cup warm water

2¼ teaspoons active dry yeast

¼ teaspoon ground nutmeg

4½ cups unbleached all-purpose flour, divided

¼ cup lard or butter

1 cup mashed potatoes

½ teaspoon salt

2 eggs, beaten

¾ cup unsalted butter, softened, divided

1 teaspoon ground cinnamon

½ cup granulated sugar

½ cup firmly packed brown sugar

½ cup chopped pecans

1. Heat milk in a saucepan until steaming and bubbles form around the edges; do not boil. Stir in ¼ cup sugar; set aside to cool to lukewarm.

2. Combine warm water and yeast in a large bowl; stir until dissolved. Stir in cooled milk mixture and nutmeg. Beat in 2 cups of flour until the mixture is a smooth batter. Cover with plastic wrap or a clean cloth and let rise in a warm place.

3. In a medium bowl, beat lard or butter and remaining sugar on medium-high speed for 3 minutes. Blend in mashed potatoes. Stir in salt and eggs. Blend mixture into yeast mixture. Mix in remaining 2½ cups flour. Place dough in a greased bowl. Cover and let rise until doubled in size.

4. Turn dough onto a lightly floured work surface. Roll to a ¼-inch-thick rectangle, 15 inches wide by any length. Using a rubber spatula, spread ½ cup (1 stick) of the softened butter evenly over the dough, leaving a ½-inch border; combine the cinnamon and sugar in a small bowl and sprinkle over the butter layer. Roll up jellyroll-style, pressing edges firmly, and moisten the top edge with water to seal the roll. Using a sharp knife (or unflavored, unwaxed dental floss), cut into 1-inch-thick slices.

5. Melt the remaining ¼ cup of butter in a 9 x 13-inch baking pan. Sprinkle in the brown sugar and pecans. Place the sliced rolls close together, cut side down, in the pan. Let rise until doubled in size.

6. Bake at 350°F for about 25 minutes. Invert pan on a serving plate so the caramelized brown sugar and pecans are on top. Serve warm or cooled.

ICED CINNAMON ROLLS

These cinnamon rolls use an old-fashioned but time-honored method of first making a sponge dough, which allows the dough to ferment and build extra flavor before being combined with the rest of the ingredients. These are large, bakery-style rolls, and the buttermilk icing is irresistible.

A decidedly modern trick for slicing the dough roll: Use unflavored, unwaxed dental floss to cleanly cut the dough into rounds. It's light enough to allow you to slice through the soft dough without squeezing out the filling.
Yields 12 rolls

INGREDIENTS

2¼ teaspoons active dry yeast

1 teaspoon salt

2 cups lukewarm water

8½ to 9½ cups unbleached all-purpose flour, divided

1 cup granulated sugar

1 cup lard or unsalted butter, chilled

1 egg plus 2 egg yolks

½ cup cold water

½ cup unsalted butter, softened

¾ cup firmly packed brown sugar

2 tablespoons ground cinnamon

ICING

3 tablespoons cream cheese, softened

3 tablespoons buttermilk or sour milk (see page 40)

1½ cups powdered sugar

¼ teaspoon vanilla extract

1. In a large bowl, combine the yeast, salt, lukewarm water, and 4 cups of flour. With a large rubber spatula, mix together thoroughly; the dough will be very sticky. Cover with plastic wrap or a lint-free cotton or linen tea towel (terry cloth will stick and leave lint on the dough) and set in a warm place to rise for 2 hours. (This is the sponge.)

2. In a separate large bowl, cream together the sugar and lard (or butter); add 2 cups of flour, one at a time, stirring well after each addition; mixture will resemble pie dough.

3. In a small bowl, beat the egg and yolks with an electric mixer on medium-high speed until foamy, about 1 minute. Add the cold water to the eggs and stir to combine. Combine the 3 mixtures all at once in the sponge bowl and beat on low speed until smooth. Add enough additional flour (up to 2½ cups) to make the dough similar to the consistency of bread dough. Cover with plastic wrap or a lint-free cotton or linen tea towel and set in a warm place to rise, about 1½ to 2 hours.

4. When doubled in size, turn dough onto a floured board and knead until soft and pliable, about 10 minutes, adding up to 1 cup more of flour.

5. Roll out the dough to a 16 x 12-inch rectangle ⅓ inch thick with a long side facing you. Using a rubber spatula, spread the softened butter evenly over the dough, leaving a ½-inch border at the far end. Combine the brown sugar and cinnamon in a small bowl and mix with a fork. Sprinkle the mixture evenly over the butter layer.

6. Grease two 13 x 9-inch baking dishes with lard or butter.

7. Starting with the long side closest to you, roll up the dough like a jellyroll, pinching with your fingertips as you roll. Moisten the top edge with water to seal the roll.

8. Using a sharp knife (or dental floss, see recipe introduction), cut the roll into 12 equal slices; place 6 rolls, cut side down, close together in each dish. Cover loosely with plastic wrap or a

cotton or linen tea towel and set in a warm place to rise until doubled, about 1½ to 2 hours.

9. Adjust the oven racks to the upper-middle and lower-middle positions. Preheat oven to 350°F. Bake both dishes at the same time for 25 to 30 minutes until golden brown; switch positions of the dishes halfway through the baking time. Remove from the oven and let cool on a wire rack for 5 minutes.

10. To prepare the icing, place the cream cheese, buttermilk, and half the sugar in a large bowl and beat with an electric mixer until smooth and free of lumps. Add the remaining sugar and the vanilla and beat. Using a tablespoon, drizzle the icing evenly over the rolls. Serve warm.

YORKSHIRE PUDDING

No Christmas dinner is complete without bread, and a traditional English Christmas dinner calls for Yorkshire pudding, a roll of sorts. The first documented recipe for this English dish may have been in 1737 and was called "dripping pudding," which refers to the pan drippings from roasted meat. This incredibly light and crisp puff "pudding" is a perfect accompaniment to mashed potatoes and gravy. **Yields 6 servings**

INGREDIENTS

¼ cup roast drippings or melted lard

2 eggs

1 cup milk

1 cup sifted all-purpose flour

2 teaspoons baking powder

½ teaspoon salt

1. Pour the drippings or melted lard into a 9 x 9-inch square baking pan or 6-cavity muffin/popover pan; set aside. Preheat oven to 425°F.

2. In a large bowl, beat eggs on medium-high speed until frothy. Add milk; blend well. Add flour, baking powder, and salt. Beat until smooth.

3. Place the pan with drippings in the preheated oven and heat for 5 minutes. Remove hot pan and divide the batter evenly into the 6 cavities or make 6 dollops of batter in the baking pan.

4. Bake for 30 to 35 minutes, until pudding is golden brown and puffy. Edges should be crusty. Serve hot with pot roast. Pudding will fall in the middle as it cools.

POPOVERS

A popover is the American version of Yorkshire pudding, a light, hollow, buttery roll made from an egg batter and baked in muffin pans or special straight-sided (versus angled) popover pans. The name "popover" comes from the way the batter rises or "pops" over the top of the pan while baking. For best results, follow this recipe exactly. Do not add baking powder or more flour. The batter must be thin. **Yields 12 servings**

INGREDIENTS

2 eggs

1 cup milk

½ teaspoon salt

1 cup all-purpose flour

1. Preheat oven to 375°F. Grease a standard muffin pan or popover pan; set aside.

2. In a medium bowl, beat eggs until creamy; add milk, salt, and flour, beating until smooth. Fill each muffin cavity half full with batter. Bake for 35 minutes.

3. Popovers will rise to five times original bulk and will be hollow.

Quick Breads

Quick breads are the perfect introduction to bread making. Why? Because they are easy, unintimidating, and require no special equipment or ingredients.

Quick breads act like a stepping-stone for bakers new to the craft. They do not require yeast for leavening, so their ease of preparation makes them beginner-friendly. Since quick breads depend on baking powder and baking soda to rise, a large time commitment isn't necessary. A simple blending of ingredients, adding wet to dry—sometimes in just the right order—is all that's needed to turn out a beautiful, dense golden-brown loaf of quick bread.

These recipes allow us to put a hunk of homemade goodness on the table without having to spend all day doing it. They are a beacon from the past that calls out to us in our busy lives today. We've selected the best recipes from our archives—those that call for whole grains, healthy fats, and natural sweeteners in particular—to encourage you to truly embrace "homemade" in every sense of the word. The comforting act of baking is right here in these recipes for your pleasure, so let the irresistible aromas fill your kitchen without taxing your skills or your budget.

GLAZED ORANGE-PECAN BREAD

Thanksgiving breads usually include Parker House rolls, crescents, biscuits, or whatever the regional favorite. In the South, sweet quick breads are popular, and this flavorful, aromatic loaf is sure to complement any feast, whether it's brunch, a tailgate, or a celebratory meal. **Yields 1 loaf**

INGREDIENTS

¼ cup unsalted butter, softened

¾ cup granulated sugar

2 eggs, beaten

2 teaspoons orange zest

2 cups all-purpose flour

2½ teaspoons baking powder

1 teaspoon salt

¾ cup plus 2½ teaspoons orange juice, divided

½ cup chopped pecans, plus extra for sprinkling

½ cup sifted powdered sugar

1. Preheat oven to 350°F. Grease a 9 x 5-inch loaf pan; set aside.

2. In a large bowl, beat the butter on medium speed, gradually adding the sugar, beating for a total of 3 minutes. Add eggs and orange zest; mix well.

3. In a separate bowl, combine flour, baking powder, and salt. Add to the creamed mixture in batches, alternating with ¾ cup orange juice. Begin and end with the flour mixture, mixing well after each addition. Stir in pecans.

4. Pour batter into the prepared pan and bake for 50 to 55 minutes, until a toothpick inserted in the center comes out clean.

5. Cool in pan for 10 minutes, then turn out and cool completely on a wire rack.

6. Combine remaining 2½ teaspoons orange juice with powdered sugar; whisk to blend. Drizzle over the cooled loaf. Sprinkle a tablespoon of finely chopped pecans, if desired.

7. Wrap in foil and store overnight before serving, which improves the flavor and texture.

APPLE QUICK BREAD

Apples, nuts, and honey produce this standout loaf that is delicious and healthy due to the absence of any refined sugar. Honey will render a softer bread, and it also contributes to a longer shelf life. A little toasting and some butter and cinnamon will more than do the trick for breakfast. **Yields 2 loaves**

INGREDIENTS

3 cups all-purpose flour

1 teaspoon baking soda

½ teaspoon baking powder

1 teaspoon salt

1½ cups milk

1 cup honey

2 eggs

1 tablespoon vanilla extract

2 cups peeled and finely diced Granny Smith apples (or other tart apple)

1 cup finely chopped pecans

1. Preheat oven to 350°F. Grease two 9 x 5-inch loaf pans; set aside.

2. In a medium bowl, combine flour, baking soda, baking powder, and salt. Set aside.

3. In a large bowl, whisk together milk, honey, eggs, and vanilla. Fold in dry ingredients until just blended. Stir in apples and pecans.

4. Divide batter between the two prepared pans. Bake for about 45 minutes, until a toothpick inserted in the center comes out clean.

5. Cool in pans for 15 minutes, then turn out and cool completely on a wire rack. Serve with butter and honey, if desired. Store leftovers in a plastic bag.

PUMPKIN BREAD

This sweet bread is only as flavorful as the fruit you use to prepare it. Find a *small* pie pumpkin that's been field ripened and has thick, dark flesh. Wash and dry the outside, then cleave it in half and carefully scoop out the seeds. Place both halves (cut sides down) on a baking sheet and bake at 350°F for about an hour, or until the meat is *very* soft (you can test it with a fork) and the rind is somewhat browned. After the pieces cool, scrape the pulp from the shells with a spoon and purée it in a blender (or put it through a food mill). Now the pumpkin is ready to be used in this recipe. **Yields 1 loaf**

INGREDIENTS

1 egg

1 cup pure maple syrup

½ cup virgin coconut oil, melted

1 teaspoon vanilla extract

1 cup puréed pumpkin or butternut squash

2 cups whole wheat flour

¼ teaspoon salt

¼ teaspoon baking soda

½ teaspoon baking powder

1 teaspoon ground cinnamon

½ teaspoon ground cloves

½ teaspoon ground nutmeg

⅔ cup chopped raisins

⅔ cup chopped nuts (your choice)

1. Preheat oven to 350°F. Grease a 9 x 5-inch loaf pan and dust it lightly with whole wheat flour; set aside.

2. In a large mixing bowl, blend the egg, maple syrup, oil, and vanilla. Add the 1 cup of cooked, puréed pumpkin, and beat the ingredients well.

3. In a separate bowl, mix the flour, salt, baking soda, baking powder, cinnamon, cloves, and nutmeg. Stir the wet ingredients into the dry ingredients, then add the raisins and chopped nuts.

4. Pour the batter into the pan and bake for 45 minutes; turn the oven temperature down to 300°F and bake for another 45 minutes. Cool the bread completely in the pan on a wire rack before turning it out and slicing.

BANANA NUT BREAD

You'll need four or five *very* ripe bananas to make this delicious loaf, so it's best to keep the fruit at room temperature for several days *before* you plan to make it. Microwave the bananas for a minute or two to release their sweet liquor, then mash it all together. Whole wheat flour and pure maple syrup in this recipe make for a fiber-rich and healthier loaf, minus any refined sugar. **Yields 1 loaf**

INGREDIENTS

⅓ cup unsalted butter, softened

1 egg

1 cup maple syrup

1 cup mashed bananas

2 cups whole wheat flour

3 teaspoons baking powder

½ teaspoon baking soda

½ teaspoon salt

1 cup chopped walnuts

1. Preheat oven to 350°F. Grease a 9 x 5-inch loaf pan; set aside.

2. In a large bowl, cream the butter with the egg and maple syrup. Once well blended, add the mashed bananas and mix well.

3. In a separate bowl, stir together the whole wheat flour, baking powder, baking soda, and salt. Slowly stir the banana mixture into the flour and add the chopped walnuts.

4. Pour the batter into the prepared pan. For a more even loaf, use a knife to mound the batter slightly around the edges of the pan (since it tends to rise faster in the center).

5. Bake for 25 minutes; reduce oven temperature to 300°F and bake for another 30 minutes, until a toothpick inserted into the center comes out clean. Allow the bread to cool in the pan on a wire rack completely before turning it out and slicing.

CRANBERRY NUT BREAD

This is a tart and tasty holiday treat, perfect for Thanksgiving or Christmas. Youngsters may be dubious about the "new" dessert at first, but after one slice, they'll attack the bread with such enthusiasm that you'll probably have to make another loaf before the holidays are over! **Yields 1 loaf**

INGREDIENTS

2 cups whole wheat flour

1 tablespoon baking powder

1 teaspoon baking soda

1 teaspoon salt

¼ cup unsalted butter, chilled and cubed

1 egg

¾ cup orange juice

½ cup honey

½ cup chopped walnuts

1 cup chopped fresh cranberries

1. Preheat oven to 350°F. Grease a 9 x 5-inch loaf pan; set aside.

2. In a large bowl, mix together the flour, baking powder, baking soda, and salt. Using a pastry blender or two knives, cut in the butter until the mixture resembles coarse meal.

3. In a small bowl, beat the egg and blend in the orange juice and honey. Pour the liquids all at once into the dry ingredients and stir only enough to blend everything well. Fold in the chopped walnuts and cranberries.

4. Pour the batter into the prepared pan. For a more even loaf, use a knife to mound the batter slightly around the edges of the pan (since it tends to rise faster in the center).

5. Bake for 1 hour, until a toothpick inserted in the center comes out clean. Cool in pan on a wire rack completely before turning out and slicing.

SQUASH, WHOLE WHEAT, AND PECAN BREAD

If you love to create new recipes using produce from your garden, give this recipe a try; it's a reader's delightful substitution for zucchini bread. Instead of zucchini and walnuts, she uses pattypan squash and pecans, and the results are certainly worth the effort. However, if you happen to be growing zucchini squash, feel free to substitute it for the pattypan. **Yields 2 loaves**

INGREDIENTS

3 cups whole wheat flour (or use 1½ cups all-purpose and 1½ cups whole wheat for a lighter bread)

1 teaspoon salt

1 teaspoon baking soda

1 teaspoon baking powder

3½ teaspoons ground cinnamon

1 teaspoon ground nutmeg

3 eggs

½ cup unsalted butter, melted

½ cup sour cream

3 teaspoons vanilla extract

2 cups sugar

3 cups grated pattypan squash

1½ cups chopped pecans

1. Preheat oven to 325°F. Grease and flour two 8 x 4-inch loaf pans; set aside.

2. In a large bowl, sift together the flour, salt, baking soda, baking powder, cinnamon, and nutmeg.

3. In a separate bowl, beat the eggs, melted butter, sour cream, vanilla, and sugar. Add sifted ingredients and beat well. Stir in squash and pecans until thoroughly combined.

4. Pour batter evenly into prepared pans. Bake for 50 to 70 minutes, until a toothpick inserted in the center comes out clean. Cool in the pans on a rack for 20 minutes. Remove loaves from pans and allow to cool completely before turning out and slicing.

CHOCOLATE ZUCCHINI BREAD

Chocolate plus zucchini is a win-win situation in our book. Garden produce loaded with nutrition and fiber plus the delicious benefits of dark chocolate—we don't believe it gets much better than that. This bread makes a sweet gift for that gardening neighbor who always bequeaths zucchini to the neighborhood, and this recipe makes two loaves—plenty to share. **Yields 2 loaves**

INGREDIENTS

2 cups all-purpose flour

2 cups sugar

1 teaspoon salt

2 teaspoons baking soda

¼ teaspoon baking powder

¾ cup cocoa powder

3 cups grated zucchini, patted dry

3 eggs

½ cup virgin coconut oil or 1½ cups applesauce

¾ cup dark or bittersweet chocolate chips (optional)

1. Preheat oven to 350°F. Grease two 9 x 5-inch loaf pans; set aside.

2. In a large bowl, combine flour, sugar, salt, baking soda, baking powder, and cocoa. In a separate bowl, combine zucchini, eggs, and oil or applesauce; mix well. Add wet ingredients to dry and mix well. Stir in chocolate chips if using.

3. Divide batter evenly into the prepared pans and bake for 45 minutes to 1 hour, until a toothpick inserted in the center comes out clean. Cool loaves on a wire rack completely before turning out.

4. Variation: Use 3 teaspoons cinnamon and 2 teaspoons vanilla extract in place of cocoa, and omit the chocolate chips.

BOSTON BROWN BREAD

This traditional brown bread is baked in repurposed aluminum or tin cans, such as a coffee can, as was the custom in the 1950s. If you're concerned about the safety of baking in such cans (or getting the finished product out of the can), you can steam this bread in a traditional loaf pan (8 x 4-inch) or medium-size pudding mold. **Yields 2 loaves**

INGREDIENTS

2 cups all-purpose flour

2 teaspoons salt

2 teaspoons baking soda

2 cups bran cereal

1 cup sugar

1½ cups raisins

2½ tablespoons molasses

2 cups buttermilk or sour milk (see page 40)

1. In a large bowl, sift together the flour, salt, and baking soda. Add the cereal, sugar, and raisins.

2. In another bowl, combine molasses and buttermilk. Add to the dry ingredients and mix well.

3. Heat a large pan of water. Grease or spray two 15-ounce tin cans. Pour mixture into cans and top with wax paper.

4. Place cans in the hot water (water should come halfway up the cans) and steam for approximately 2½ hours; begin timing when water comes to a boil. Water should be kept at a slow rolling boil and replenished if needed. Remove cans from the water when a toothpick inserted in the center comes out clean. Cool on a wire rack for 10 minutes, then unmold and cool completely. Store leftovers in the refrigerator.

ESTHER SHUTTLEWORTH'S BEER BREAD

Esther Shuttleworth was a woman who worked night and day on her homestead, building some security for her family. After a long day of working your farm (especially in cold weather), Esther's beer bread is a quick and welcomed addition to any meal. **Yields 2 to 3 loaves**

INGREDIENTS

3 cups self-rising flour

2 tablespoons sugar

12 ounces beer

½ cup unsalted butter, melted

1. Preheat oven to 350°F. Grease two or three loaf pans (use two for thicker loaves); set aside.

2. In a large bowl, combine the flour and sugar. Add beer gradually while mixing. Pour the batter evenly into the prepared pans and drizzle the melted butter over the top; the butter should form a ⅛-inch layer over the dough.

3. Bake for about 50 minutes, until a toothpick inserted in the center comes out clean. Cool on a wire rack completely before turning out.

Tip: You can substitute 1 tablespoon of honey for the 2 tablespoons of sugar; if so, also decrease the amount of beer by 1 tablespoon. This is also delicious with fresh or dried herbs.

HERB AND CHEESE BREAD

This delicious cheesy bread can double as a pizza crust. It's not time consuming like traditional pizza crust, so it works in a pinch. To make a pizza, bake the recipe in a pie pan; when it comes out of the oven, just add some pizza sauce, cheese, and whatever toppings your family happens to like, then put it back in the oven just long enough to melt the cheese. It makes an easy, tasty meal. **Yields 1 loaf**

INGREDIENTS

1¼ cups all-purpose flour

1½ tablespoons baking powder

½ teaspoon baking soda

Pinch black pepper

1½ teaspoons sugar

1 egg

⅔ cup buttermilk or sour milk (see page 40)

1½ to 2 tablespoons olive oil

⅓ cup freshly grated Parmesan cheese

⅓ cup grated part-skim provolone or mozzarella cheese

2 tablespoons chopped fresh Italian parsley

1 teaspoon chopped fresh basil

1 teaspoon chopped fresh thyme

1 teaspoon chopped fresh oregano

½ teaspoon chopped fresh savory

1. Preheat oven to 350°F. Grease an 8½ x 4½–inch loaf pan; set aside.

2. In a mixing bowl, combine flour, baking powder, baking soda, pepper, and sugar.

3. Add egg, buttermilk, and oil, and stir until just blended. Stir in cheeses and herbs, mixing until just blended.

4. Pour into the prepared pan. Bake for 45 minutes until light golden brown. Cool in pan for 5 minutes, then turn onto a wire rack. Serve warm.

Flatbreads & Crackers

. . . .

The different variations of flatbreads found all over the world are generally made with flour, water, and salt and then thoroughly rolled into flattened dough. After that, the differences abound. From the tortillas of Mexico and South America to the pizza crusts and focaccia of Europe to the naan and pita of the Middle and South East to the chapati of Africa and India, there is a specialty flatbread to suit every palate!

Some flatbreads are cooked on a skillet or griddle until brown speckles appear; others are baked in the oven until puffed and golden brown. Some flatbreads are soft and pliable, making them excellent for wraps and scoops, while others are firm and can be dipped in olive oil or sliced and used for the base of a sandwich. Flatbreads are delicious and easy to make (sometimes requiring no rising time), making them a perfect accompaniment to weeknight suppers.

We've included recipes for just about all the major flatbreads of the world, including some not-so-common variations such as Swedish hardtack and homemade graham crackers. Who knew you could make crackers at home? You'll come back to these recipes again and again as you discover the versatile world of flatbreads.

FLATBREAD I

Basic Middle Eastern–style flatbread is made with flour, water, and salt, and then thoroughly rolled into flattened dough. The dough is then cooked on a skillet or griddle until brown speckles appear. Flatbread is versatile in that it can be eaten plain, dipped in oil or butter, or used as a base for a type of rolled sandwich. **Yields 6 pieces**

INGREDIENTS

2 cups unbleached all-purpose flour

¾ cup water
½ teaspoon salt

6 teaspoons olive oil, divided
Sea salt and pepper, to taste

1. In a large bowl, combine flour, water, and salt until dough sticks together but is flaky and dry to the touch. Turn out onto a floured work surface and knead for 1 to 2 minutes. Roll dough into a 6-inch log; cut into 1-inch slices.

2. With a floured rolling pin, roll out slices as thin as you can get them; set aside.

3. Heat a 10-inch cast-iron skillet over medium heat until hot; add 1 teaspoon olive oil and swirl over bottom. Add one dough round and cook until edges have hardened and bubbles form in the center, about 60 to 70 seconds, then flip and cook the other side for the same amount of time. Repeat for each dough piece.

4. Remove from skillet and season with additional sea salt and pepper, to taste. Stack flatbread on a plate covered with a tea towel until serving time; serve warm.

FLATBREAD II

This two-ingredient, soft and pliable flatbread is so easy to make. The yogurt gives it the perfect amount of moisture; the dough is soft with a slight flakiness that cannot be achieved without yogurt. Wrap up your favorite fillings and make a sandwich with this bread. **Yields 12 pieces**

INGREDIENTS

4 cups self-rising flour
2 cups plain yogurt

Melted butter or oil, for brushing (optional)

Sea salt, for sprinkling (optional)

1. Place the ingredients in the bowl of a food processor; pulse until dough forms. If the dough is too wet, add a little additional self-rising flour.

2. Turn dough out onto a floured work surface and knead for 1 to 2 minutes, just enough to bring dough together.

3. Divide dough into 12 equal pieces. Roll each piece out thin into 4- to 5-inch-diameter rounds.

4. Heat a small dry skillet over high heat until hot. Add rounds, cooking in batches, and cook for about 2 minutes per side, turning when slightly puffy. Brush with melted butter or olive oil, plus a sprinkle of sea salt, if desired. Stack on a plate and cover with a tea towel until ready to serve.

ROSEMARY-GARLIC FLATBREAD

With the cheese, garlic, and herbs, this bread is almost a complete meal. Just add a salad and you'll have a splendid little repast. This flatbread has a lovely open crumb with a crunchy crust—very Italian. **Yields 1 piece**

INGREDIENTS

- 3 tablespoons olive oil, plus more for greasing the pan
- 3 sprigs fresh rosemary (about 2 inches each), or 1 teaspoon dried
- 3 large garlic cloves, quartered
- 1 to 1¼ cups warm water

- 2¼ teaspoons active dry yeast
- 1 tablespoon honey
- 1 cup unbleached all-purpose or bread flour
- 1 to 1¼ cups whole wheat flour
- 1 teaspoon salt

- 1 cup finely shredded provolone or asiago cheese
- 1 tablespoon chopped fresh rosemary, or 1 teaspoon dried

1. Place the olive oil, rosemary sprigs, and garlic in a small saucepan, and warm over medium-low heat for 5 minutes, until the garlic just begins to sizzle. Turn off the heat; set aside.

2. Place 1 cup warm water in a large bowl and sprinkle the yeast on top. Add honey, stir to blend, and then add the bread flour. Mix well, adding more water if necessary, and set aside for 30 minutes.

3. Remove the rosemary and garlic from the oil. Discard the rosemary and coarsely chop the garlic; set aside. Add the salt and half the scented olive oil to the yeast mixture, stir, and then add the whole wheat flour. Stir well for 2 minutes (the

dough will be quite sticky). Cover with a damp cloth, and set to rise in a warm, draft-free place for 45 minutes.

4. Oil a baking sheet with olive oil. Oil your hands with the remaining scented oil, and gently shape the dough into a ball. Place it on the prepared sheet and press to form a ½-inch-thick oval, about 12 inches wide and 14 inches long. Sprinkle the cheese evenly over the top, followed by the garlic and chopped fresh rosemary. Let rise for 30 minutes.

5. Preheat oven to 400°F. Bake for 20 minutes, until lightly browned. Allow to cool for a few minutes before serving.

FLOUR TORTILLAS I

Yields 12 pieces

INGREDIENTS

3 cups unbleached all-purpose flour

2 teaspoons baking powder

1 teaspoon salt

4 to 6 tablespoons lard, chilled and coarsely chopped

1¼ cups warm water

1. In a large bowl, combine the flour, baking powder, and salt. Using a pastry blender or two knives, cut in the lard until the mixture resembles coarse meal.

2. Add the warm water a little at a time until the dough is soft and no longer sticky.

3. Turn the dough onto a floured work surface and knead for a few minutes until it's soft and pliable. Divide the dough evenly into 12 golf ball–size pieces. Cover with a cloth and let the dough rest for 10 minutes or longer.

4. Dust each ball with flour and roll out with a rolling pin or *palote* (tortilla rolling pin) as thinly as possible without tearing (¹⁄₁₆ inch or thinner).

5. Heat a griddle, *comal* (tortilla griddle), or cast-iron skillet over medium-high heat. (Do not use a very hot griddle or the tortillas will cook too quickly.)

6. One at a time, lay a tortilla on the hot griddle. Let it brown for a few seconds on one side, then turn it over. Each side should be nicely speckled.

7. After browning, place the tortilla on a towel or in a tortilla warmer and cover. Serve warm.

FLOUR TORTILLAS II

Yields 8 pieces

INGREDIENTS

2 cups unbleached all-purpose flour

½ teaspoon salt

¾ cup water

3 tablespoons olive oil

1. In a large bowl, combine flour and salt. Stir in water and oil, mixing to form dough.

2. Turn dough onto a floured work surface and knead for 1 to 2 minutes, until dough is smooth. (If dough is too dry, add a little more water; if too wet, add a little additional flour.) Let dough rest for 10 minutes.

3. Divide dough into 8 equal pieces. Using a floured rolling pin, roll each piece into a 7-inch-diameter circle.

4. Heat a skillet or griddle over medium heat until hot. Add a dash of oil to the pan. Add tortillas, 1 or 2 at a time, and cook for about 1 minute on each side, turning once. Both sides should be lightly browned when tortillas are done. Be careful not to burn them. Remove from skillet and keep warm while cooking remaining tortillas.

CHEWY SEMOLINA PIZZA CRUST

Semolina is the coarse, purified wheat middlings of durum wheat. (Durum flour is the fine grind.) With its sand-like consistency, semolina flour imparts a light flavor and airy texture to baked goods. This pizza crust is thick and chewy, with delightful semolina flavor. If you've never used semolina flour, this is an excellent recipe to start with. **Yields 2 large crusts**

INGREDIENTS

1¼ cups warm water (105–115°F)

1 teaspoon honey

2½ teaspoons active dry yeast

1¾ cups semolina flour

1½ cups unbleached all-purpose flour

¾ teaspoon salt

Olive oil, for brushing

1. In the bowl of a stand mixer, combine water, honey, and yeast. Let stand for 5 minutes, or until yeast is foamy.

2. Stir in flours and salt. Knead with dough hook for 4 to 5 minutes, until dough is smooth yet still sticky. Shape dough into a ball and put into an oiled bowl, turning once to coat all sides. Cover with plastic wrap or a lint-free cotton or linen tea towel (terry cloth will stick and leave lint on the dough) and let rise in a warm spot for 45 to 60 minutes.

3. Turn dough onto a lightly floured work surface. Punch down and divide into two equal parts. If you do not intend to use both crusts, place leftover dough in a plastic bag and refrigerate for up to 2 days or freeze for up to 1 month.

TO BAKE

4. Preheat oven to 500°F. Rub olive oil generously on a heavy baking sheet or round pizza pan.

5. Using your fingers, press out the dough roughly into an 8 x 6-inch rectangle or to partially cover the baking vessel. Brush with olive oil. Cover and let rest for about 15 minutes.

6. After dough has rested, roll or press it out to fit prepared pan entirely. Spoon on the sauce, followed by desired toppings. Bake for 12 to 13 minutes, or until crust is golden brown and cheese is bubbling.

7. Slide pizza off baking pan onto a cutting board and cut to serve.

CRISPY PIZZA CRUST

If you're a fan of thin, crispy pizza crust, this is the perfect recipe for you. It's easy to make and rolls out beautifully without tearing. Use one crust tonight and freeze the other for next week. **Yields 2 large crusts**

INGREDIENTS

2½ cups unbleached all-purpose flour

1½ teaspoons quick-rise yeast

1 teaspoon salt

¾ cup warm water (105–115°F)

2 teaspoons honey

3 tablespoons olive oil

1. In the bowl of a stand mixer, combine flour, yeast, and salt. Stir in water, honey, and olive oil until combined. Set to knead with the dough-hook attachment for about 6 minutes, until dough is smooth and satiny.

2. Shape dough into a ball and place in an oiled bowl, turning once to coat all sides. Cover and set in a warm spot to rise for about 1½ hours.

3. Turn dough onto a lightly floured work surface. Punch down and divide into two equal parts. If you do not intend to use both crusts, place leftover dough in a plastic bag and refrigerate for up to 2 days or freeze for up to 1 month.

4. Place dough on oiled baking sheet or cutting board to rest for 10 minutes.

TO BAKE

5. Preheat oven and baking stone, pizza pan, or baking sheet to 500°F.

6. Sprinkle dough with flour and, based on the shape of the pan you're using, roll out to a 9 x 13-inch rectangle or 12-inch circle about ¹⁄₁₆ inch thick.

7. Drape dough over the rolling pin and transfer to the preheated vessel, carefully unrolling it and being careful not to burn yourself.

8. Quickly spread sauce over crust, followed by desired toppings.

9. Bake for 8 to 10 minutes, until crust is browned and cheese is bubbling.

CRUNCHY CORNMEAL PIZZA CRUST

This delicious crust is a little bit crunchy, and a whole lot of flavorful. You can use any combination of flour in this crust—all white, all whole wheat, or 2 cups whole wheat and 1 cup of something else: all-purpose, spelt flour, and so on. It turns out best when you use at least 1 cup white flour, but it's fun to make it your own, and you never know what might happen with your own favorite flours. **Yields 2 large crusts**

INGREDIENTS

1 cup warm water (105–115°F)

1½ teaspoons active dry yeast

½ teaspoon honey

2 tablespoons olive oil

1 cup whole wheat flour

2 cups unbleached all-purpose flour

¼ cup cornmeal

1¼ teaspoons salt

1. In the bowl of a stand mixer, whisk together the water, yeast, and honey; set aside for 10 minutes to proof. When surface appears foamy, add oil and stir.

2. In a separate bowl, whisk together the flours, cornmeal, and salt. Add to liquid mixture and knead with dough hook for about 5 minutes, until dough is soft and pliable.

3. Transfer dough to an oiled bowl and turn once to coat all sides. Cover with plastic wrap or a lint-free cotton or linen tea towel (terry cloth will stick and leave lint on the dough) and set in a warm spot to rise until doubled or tripled in size, about 1½ to 2 hours.

4. Punch down dough and divide into two equal portions, refrigerating or freezing portions you don't plan to use within 2 days.

TO BAKE

5. Preheat oven and baking stone or pan to 475°F. Roll out dough into a thin round to fit your pan or stone. Fold dough over a rolling pin and carefully transfer to the hot pan.

6. Quickly spoon sauce over crust and add desired toppings.

7. Bake for 12 to 15 minutes, until browned and bubbling. Slide pizza off baking pan onto a cutting board and cut to serve.

CAST-IRON SKILLET PIZZA CRUST

This delightful recipe is easy as pie to bring together for supper, requiring no extensive mixing, kneading, or rise times—and who doesn't have a cast-iron skillet to put to use here? The crust will be a little firmer and hold up to toppings better if bread flour is used. **Yields 1 medium crust**

INGREDIENTS

1 teaspoon active dry yeast

⅓ cup warm or room-temperature water

¾ cup unbleached all-purpose or bread flour

½ teaspoon salt

¾ teaspoon sugar

sauce, cheese, and toppings of your choice

1. In a small cup, combine the yeast and water and let sit for 10 minutes, until foamy. In a large bowl, mix the flour, salt, and sugar. Stir in the yeast mixture.

2. Stir it until well mixed. The dough should be thick, requiring a little effort to mix it. Cover the bowl with plastic wrap or a lint-free cotton or linen tea towel (terry cloth will stick and leave lint on the dough) and let rise in a warm or room-temperature place for about 2 hours. Grease a 10-inch cast-iron skillet if it's not already well seasoned.

3. After the dough has risen, turn onto a floured work surface. Knead for 5 to 10 minutes until smooth and less sticky.

4. Preheat oven to 425°F.

5. With a rolling pin, roll dough into a round shape and lift it into the pan, or push the dough into place in the pan with your fingers. The edges should come up a little on the side of the pan to form a rim. Add sauce and toppings.

6. Bake for about 15 minutes, until the cheese bubbles up and the top browns.

7. Slide the pizza out of the pan onto a cutting board and cut into slices.

ROSEMARY FOCACCIA

Focaccia is an oven-baked Italian flatbread that calls for much more leavening than pizza dough, resulting in a higher-rising bread. Focaccia has a firm crust with an airy crumb that has the ability to absorb large amounts of olive oil and is sometimes known as "olive oil bread." This recipe calls for a little whole wheat flour, but you can use all white flour for a traditional Italian-style bread. **Yields 1 large piece**

FOCACCIA

2 teaspoons active dry yeast

1½ cups warm water, 100–105°F, divided

3½ cups unbleached all-purpose flour

½ cup whole wheat flour

2 tablespoons olive oil

1 teaspoon salt

2 tablespoons fresh minced rosemary

Cornmeal, for the baking sheet

TOPPINGS

2 cloves garlic, minced

About 5 tablespoons olive oil, divided

1 generous tablespoon fresh minced rosemary

1 medium onion, quartered lengthwise and thinly sliced

Coarse sea salt

About ½ cup pitted kalamata olives (optional)

1. In a cup, combine yeast and ¼ cup warm water; let sit until foamy, about 10 minutes.

2. In a large bowl, mix the flours and make a well in the center. Pour yeast mixture and about half the remaining water into the well; stir gently. Add olive oil, salt, and rest of water and stir to blend.

3. Turn dough onto a lightly floured work surface. Gather the dough and knead it, adding more flour if necessary. Sprinkle rosemary over the dough, fold over, and knead rosemary into the dough. Dough should be soft and pliable after 7 to 8 minutes.

4. Transfer dough to a lightly oiled bowl and let rest until doubled in bulk. (Ideally, this should be done in the refrigerator overnight, but it is not necessary.)

5. Punch dough down and pat it into a rough rectangle with your hands. Let rest, covered with a towel, for 20 minutes, or until dough is at room temperature if it has been refrigerated.

6. Lightly sprinkle cornmeal on a baking sheet. Transfer dough to baking sheet and stretch gently with your hands. Cover with a towel and let dough rise in a warm place for about 15 minutes.

7. Place a baking stone on the bottom rack of the oven and preheat oven and baking stone to 450°F.

8. Once focaccia dough has risen on the baking sheet, spread your fingers wide and gently press down on dough to make indentations all over the top.

9. To assemble toppings: Place garlic in shallow dish and add about 3 tablespoons olive oil. Brush dough with olive oil and garlic, letting some collect in depressions. Sprinkle rosemary over dough and spread onion over top of focaccia.

10. Place baking sheet directly on baking stone or on middle rack of oven. Bake for about 25 minutes. When focaccia is done, it will be golden brown on edges and crisp on outside. Remove from oven and brush with remaining olive oil, especially on outer edges. Sprinkle generously with coarse salt. Garnish with olives, if desired. Cut and serve warm.

HOMEMADE NAAN

Naan is a leavened, oven-baked flatbread traditionally cooked in a tandoor—a cylindrical clay oven heated with charcoal or wood—found in the cuisines of West, Central, and South Asia, and believed to have originated in Persia. This soft, flexible flatbread is used to scoop meat and/or sauces and can be brushed with oil, ghee, or butter. **Yields 16 pieces**

INGREDIENTS

2¼ teaspoons active dry yeast

1 cup warm water

¼ cup sugar

3 tablespoons milk

1 egg, slightly beaten

2 teaspoons fine sea salt

4¼ cups bread flour

2 teaspoons minced garlic (about 2 cloves)

Olive oil, for the pan

¼ cup butter, melted, for brushing

1. In a large bowl, combine yeast and warm water; let stand until frothy, about 10 minutes. Stir in the sugar, milk, egg, salt, and enough flour to make a soft dough.

2. Turn dough onto a floured work surface and knead until smooth, 6 to 8 minutes. Transfer dough to an oiled bowl and turn to coat; cover with a damp towel, and let rise for about 1 hour, until doubled in size.

3. Punch down the dough, then knead in the minced garlic for 1 to 2 minutes, just until incorporated. Pinch off bits of dough and roll into balls the size of golf balls. Set balls on a lightly floured surface and cover with a towel; let rise until doubled in size, about 30 to 40 minutes.

4. Heat a skillet or griddle over medium-high heat until hot. Add a little oil to the pan.

5. Roll each dough ball into a ⅛-inch-thick circle. Cook each circle for 2 to 3 minutes, until the bottom is lightly browned and the top is puffy. Brush the top with melted butter, then flip and brush the browned side with butter. Continue cooking for 2 to 4 minutes, or until bottom is lightly browned like the top. Remove and stack on a plate, covered with a towel, while cooking the remaining dough.

YOGURT NAAN

Typically associated with Indian cuisine, naan is the perfect companion to spicy meat or vegetable dishes and can be used to sop up every last morsel of sauce. The yogurt in this recipe makes a very soft dough and adds a bit of a tangy flavor. **Yields 10 pieces**

INGREDIENTS

3 cups unbleached all-purpose flour

2 teaspoons baking powder

½ teaspoon baking soda

1 teaspoon salt

1½ teaspoons sugar

⅓ cup plain yogurt

⅔ cup water

2 tablespoons olive oil

Butter, melted, for brushing

1. In a large bowl, combine the flour, baking powder, baking soda, salt, and sugar. Add yogurt, water, and oil. Mix until dough forms (it will be soft and sticky). Turn out onto a lightly floured work surface and knead for 2 minutes, until a ball forms.

2. Using kitchen scissors, cut dough into 10 equal pieces and flatten each into a disk. Sprinkle both sides of disks with additional flour and stretch disks out into small ovals.

3. Roll out a piece into a thin oval shape. Repeat with remaining dough.

4. Heat a skillet or griddle over medium-high heat until hot. Cook naan for 1 minute, until top puffs and bubbles. Flip and cook the other side for 1 minute. Repeat cooking for another minute per side, or until puffy and browned in spots.

5. Remove from griddle and brush tops with butter. Stack on a plate, covered with a towel until all pieces are cooked.

INDIAN FLATBREAD

Whole wheat flour and sesame oil give this flatbread an exotic flavor that pairs perfectly with spicy and cool toppings like chutney and sour cream. Add some sesame seeds or minced garlic to the dough for added dimension. **Yields 10 pieces**

INGREDIENTS

1 cup whole wheat flour

1 cup unbleached all-purpose flour

1 teaspoon salt

2 tablespoons sesame oil, plus more for the pan

¾ cup (more or less) hot water

1. In a large bowl, combine flours and salt. Stir in oil and enough water to make a soft dough. Dough should be elastic but not sticky. Turn out onto a floured work surface and knead until smooth.

2. Divide dough into 10 equal pieces; roll each piece into a ball and set aside to rest for 5 minutes.

3. Heat a skillet over medium heat until hot. Add a few drops of oil to the pan or coat with nonstick cooking spray.

4. Roll dough balls out very thin, into ⅛-inch-thick rounds. Cook one piece at a time until the bottom has brown spots, about 30 to 40 seconds, then flip and cook the other side. Remove and keep warm while repeating with remaining dough.

CRISPY CHAPATI

Chapati is an unleavened flatbread from India, Nepal, Bangladesh, and Pakistan. Pieces are torn off and used to pick up the meat or vegetables that make the meal. The tortilla-like chapati is traditionally folded into a loose cone and used like a utensil to eat the saucy dishes at a meal. The thickness of the chapati has a lot to do with its flavor: the thinner each one is, the more nut-like and crackery it tastes. Chapatis thicker than ¼ inch are too dense and doughy for most palates, so practice rolling the dough extra thin. **Yields 12 pieces**

INGREDIENTS

2 cups whole wheat flour

½ to 1 teaspoon salt

2 tablespoons clarified butter or cooking oil, plus extra for kneading

½ to 1 cup water

Butter, melted, or ghee, for brushing (optional)

1. Combine the flour, salt, and clarified butter or oil in a large bowl. Mix thoroughly, then gradually add ½ to 1 cup of water until the dough is smooth, elastic, and moist, but not sticky.

2. Spread a small amount of oil on a breadboard—or other work surface—to prevent sticking, and knead the dough for at least 10 minutes. (The more you knead, the lighter the chapatis.)

3. Cover and leave the dough to rest on the board for 5 minutes to an hour. When it's ready, divide the dough into roughly 12 egg-size pieces. Flatten each one with the heel of your hand, dust both sides lightly with flour, and roll the lumps into thin, round wafers, about 6 inches across. You can crank out chapatis at a pretty good clip once you get the hang of it, especially if one person rolls the dough while another cooks each disk as it comes off the assembly line.

4. Heat a dry skillet on medium heat. Cook a single chapati at a time for about 30 seconds on each side, until light-brown splotches appear (for bread flexible enough to wrap around the filling of your choice). Bake each disk longer if you want crisp, crackly wafers for tostadas or imitation tortilla chips. Brush with melted butter or ghee, if desired.

Tip: A large baking sheet placed across two burners of your gas or electric stove will increase your production. Plus you can bake more chapatis on another baking sheet in the oven at the same time (set at 350°F).

EASY PITA BREAD

Common in Mediterranean, Balkan, and Middle Eastern cuisines, pita is a soft, slightly leavened flatbread made with wheat flour. Most pitas are baked at high temperatures (450°F), which causes the dough to puff up dramatically, forming a pocket inside the bread that can be opened and filled after the bread cools. This recipe is "easy" because you cook it in a skillet on the stovetop, like the other flatbreads in this chapter. In addition to making sandwiches like gyros or meat kebabs, pita can be used to scoop sauces or dips such as hummus, or they can be cut and baked into crispy pita chips. **Yields 8 pieces**

INGREDIENTS

2 teaspoons instant yeast

1 teaspoon sugar

$\frac{2}{3}$ cup warm water

$\frac{1}{2}$ cup warm milk

1 tablespoon olive oil

1 teaspoon salt

3 to 4 cups bread flour, divided

1. In a large bowl, mix yeast, sugar, water, milk, oil, salt, and 1 cup flour until well combined. Gradually add enough remaining flour to form a soft dough that pulls away from the sides of the bowl and forms a ball. Turn dough onto a lightly floured work surface and knead until smooth, about 5 minutes.

2. Transfer dough to a lightly greased bowl and turn to coat all sides. Cover and let rise for about 1 hour, until doubled in size.

3. Divide dough into 8 equal pieces and return to the greased bowl. Cover and let dough rest for 10 to 15 minutes.

4. On a floured work surface, roll out one piece of dough into a 7- or 8-inch-diameter round about $\frac{1}{8}$ inch thick.

5. Heat a dry skillet or griddle over medium heat until hot. Add dough and cook for about 3 minutes. Flip when dough is bubbly and puffy. Cook until bottom is golden and browned in spots, about 2 to 3 minutes.

6. Repeat with remaining dough pieces. Stack on a plate and keep warm until serving. Slice in half and fill the pocket with desired fillings.

WHOLE WHEAT PITA

This version kicks up the flavor with whole wheat flour and molasses. The soy flour imparts a smoothness to the dough, balancing out the whole wheat flour and making it very easy to work with. **Yields 6 pieces**

INGREDIENTS

1 cup warm water

2¼ teaspoons active dry yeast

1 tablespoon unsulfured molasses

1 teaspoon salt

1½ cups whole wheat flour

1½ cups soy flour

Cornmeal, for sprinkling

1. In a large bowl, stir together the water, yeast, molasses, and salt; let stand for 10 minutes. Gradually mix in flours until incorporated.

2. Turn dough onto a floured work surface and knead until smooth, 2 to 3 minutes. Place dough in an oiled bowl, turning dough to coat all sides. Cover bowl and let rise for 1 hour.

3. Punch down dough and knead for 5 to 10 minutes more. Divide into 6 equal pieces.

4. On the floured work surface, roll dough pieces to ⅛ inch thick; cover and let rise for 30 minutes.

5. Preheat oven to 450°F. Place a baking sheet inside and let heat for 2 minutes. Remove baking sheet and sprinkle with a little cornmeal.

6. Place dough rounds on baking sheet and bake for 6 minutes. Remove from oven and cover baking sheet with a moist tea towel to soften pitas as they cool. Cut in half, then slit each half, if needed, to form pockets.

HOMEMADE WHEAT CRACKERS

You can vary this basic cracker recipe in dozens of ways. Instead of using 2 cups of whole wheat flour, for instance, you can use 1 cup of finely ground corn, rye, oats, buckwheat, or rice flour, and 1 cup of whole wheat flour. Alternatively, you can replace the sesame seeds with ½ cup of sunflower seeds, poppy seeds, shredded coconut, or chopped or ground nuts.

It's also possible to make herbed crackers once a week for a year without repeating a flavor if you use a little imagination. Try adding a teaspoon of dried (or a tablespoon of fresh) thyme, sage, rosemary, oregano, parsley, marjoram, chives, dill, savory, or basil to the basic cracker recipe; or chop a clove of garlic and toss that in. **Yields 12 to 24 pieces**

INGREDIENTS

2 cups whole wheat flour

1 teaspoon salt

½ cup sesame seeds

¼ cup wheat germ

¼ cup olive oil

½ cup cold water, plus more if necessary

1. In a large bowl, combine the flour, salt, sesame seeds, and wheat germ. Add the oil and mix well with a fork. Pour in the cold water, mix, and continue to add water 1 tablespoon at a time until the dough is soft and workable. Turn dough onto a lightly floured work surface and knead for at least 10 minutes (the longer, the better). Allow the dough to rest for a few minutes.

2. Preheat oven to 400°F.

3. Pinch off a golf ball–size lump of dough and roll it into a ball. Using a floured rolling pin, roll out until cardboard thin—as thin as it'll get without tearing. You should now have a cracker that's about 5 inches in diameter; or shape smaller, easier-to-handle crackers with a cookie cutter. Repeat this procedure until you've used all the remaining dough. Transfer crackers to an ungreased baking sheet.

4. Bake for 15 to 20 minutes, turning once halfway through baking time so that each side is browned. Allow the crackers to cool thoroughly on a rack before storing them in an airtight container.

RYE CRACKERS—AKA SWEDISH HARDTACK

Hardtack is a simple type of cracker or biscuit. Inexpensive to make and with a long-lasting shelf life, hardtack is used when fresh food is unavailable, whether that's on the sea, or, perhaps more practically, on the trail. These crackers are a bit more flavorful than classic hardtack thanks to the addition of buttermilk, sugar, and butter, which also shortens their shelf life. Serve with cream cheese, a slice of cucumber, and a sprig of fresh dill. Hard seeds may need to be boiled in water for one to two hours, then squeezed well to remove excess moisture, before they are added to the crackers. **Yields 24 pieces**

INGREDIENTS

2 cups buttermilk or sour milk (see page 40)

½ cup sugar

½ cup unsalted butter, melted

1 teaspoon salt

⅞ teaspoon baking soda

3 to 5 cups coarse rye flour

Caraway, sesame, fennel or other seeds if desired

1. In a large bowl, mix together the buttermilk, sugar, melted butter, salt, and baking soda. Stir in flour, one cup at a time, until you have a thick dough.

2. Turn dough onto a lightly floured work surface and roll into a ball. Cut the ball into quarters. Roll each quarter into a 1½- to 2-inch cylinder. Cut each cylinder into 6 slices. Press seeds into each side of each slice.

3. Preheat oven to 425°F. Line two baking sheets with parchment paper.

4. Sprinkle rye flour liberally on the work surface. Roll out each slice as thinly as you can—about ⅛ inch thick and about a 6-inch circle. Cut a small hole in the center of each slice. Using a thin spatula, transfer crackers carefully to the prepared baking sheets.

5. Bake for about 15 minutes, until lightly browned. The crackers will be best if you let them brown slightly, but they can quickly become too brown. Watch carefully until you get the timing right for your oven.

6. Cool on a wire rack, then store in an airtight container.

OLD-FASHIONED SODA CRACKERS

Goodbye saltines, hello homemade. It can be challenging to roll out dough so thin (⅛ inch) and transfer it, but you will definitely be a better and wiser baker for having done this recipe. Serve with a steaming bowl of your own soup or chowder, and you'll be in homemade heaven. **Yields 100 pieces**

INGREDIENTS

4½ cups unbleached all-purpose flour

½ teaspoon baking soda

½ teaspoon salt

½ cup butter or lard

1½ cups water

Kosher salt, for sprinkling

1. Preheat oven to 350°F.

2. In a large bowl, combine flour with baking soda and salt. With a pastry blender or two knives, cut in butter or lard until mixture resembles coarse meal. Add water; mix just until dry ingredients are moistened.

3. Turn dough onto a lightly floured work surface; roll to ⅛ inch thick. With a sharp knife, cut into 2-inch squares; place 1 inch apart on ungreased baking sheets. Prick two to three times with a fork, and sprinkle with kosher salt to taste.

4. Bake for 20 to 25 minutes, until lightly brown. Cool on a wire rack, then store in an airtight container.

HOMEMADE GRAHAM CRACKERS

You're in for a treat (and perhaps a challenge) if you decide to embark on the path of homemade crackers. Make these for a special "campfire and s'mores" night. Everyone will love them. **Yields 24 pieces**

INGREDIENTS

4 cups whole wheat graham flour

2 teaspoons baking powder

1 cup unsalted butter, chilled and cubed

1 egg

½ cup honey

1. In a large bowl, combine flour and baking powder. Using a pastry blender or two knives, cut in butter until mixture resembles coarse meal. Stir in the egg and honey.

2. Preheat oven to 350°F. Line a baking sheet with parchment paper.

3. Turn dough onto a lightly floured work surface. Roll out to about ¼ inch thick, then cut it into "cracker-size" (3 x 3 inches or smaller) squares. Using a thin spatula, transfer to the prepared baking sheet.

4. Bake for 15 to 20 minutes, until golden brown. Keep a close eye on them—they brown up fast. Cool on a wire rack.

Muffins & Scones

Muffins and scones are another easy way into the habit of bread making. They don't require kneading or yeast or rising time. Just mix them up and you're ready to bake. They also allow for lots of great fruit and nut ingredients that can be really hard to get right in other breads.

But just because they're easy doesn't mean they aren't special. These muffins and scones are great for tea times and holidays as well as a fast breakfast on the go. No matter the occasion, or lack thereof, recipes like Chocolate–Chocolate Chip Muffins, Lemon Poppy Seed Mini Muffins, Wild-Blackberry Scones, and Savory Sage Scones will make welcome guests.

KANSAS WHEAT-BERRY MUFFINS

Kansas is known as the Wheat State (in addition to the Sunflower State) and headquarters for *Mother Earth News*. Here, we like to grind fresh, whole, organic wheat berries into flour for the ultimate flavor and nutrition in our baked goods. Throw in some fresh blueberries and sunflower seeds from our nearby farms, and we've got a real Kansas treat on our hands. **Yields 20 muffins**

INGREDIENTS

2 eggs

½ cup unsalted butter, melted

1 cup sugar

½ teaspoon almond extract

1 cup whole wheat flour

1 cup all-purpose flour

1 teaspoon baking powder

½ teaspoon salt

2 cups fresh blueberries

¼ cup unsalted shelled sunflower seeds

1. Preheat oven to 400°F. Grease two standard muffin pans or line with paper cups; four slots should be left empty. Set aside.

2. In a mixing bowl, beat together the eggs, melted butter, sugar, and almond extract. In a separate bowl, combine flours, baking powder, and salt. Stir dry ingredients into the egg mixture just until moistened. Gently fold in blueberries and sunflower seeds. Fill muffin cups three-quarters full with batter.

3. Bake for 20 minutes, until muffins are lightly golden brown. Turn out muffins immediately onto a wire rack to cool.

FALL-HARVEST PUMPKIN MUFFINS

The aromas of fall will fill your kitchen while these autumn classics are baking in the oven. Honey, pumpkin, and walnuts provide plenty of nutrition and flavor while still satisfying your sweet tooth. Watch these muffins carefully as they bake; honey will brown faster than sugar, so don't let them reach a point of no return. **Yields 12 muffins**

INGREDIENTS

1½ cups all-purpose flour

1½ teaspoons baking powder

1 teaspoon baking soda

1½ teaspoons ground cinnamon

½ teaspoon ground ginger

¼ teaspoon ground nutmeg

¼ teaspoon salt

¼ cup unsalted butter, softened

¾ cup honey

1 egg

1 cup puréed pumpkin (see page 84)

1 cup chopped, toasted walnuts

1. Preheat oven to 350°F. Grease a standard muffin pan or line with paper cups; set aside.

2. In a medium bowl, combine flour, baking powder, baking soda, cinnamon, ginger, nutmeg, and salt; set aside.

3. Using an electric mixer, beat the butter on medium-high speed until light; beat in honey, egg, and pumpkin. Gradually add flour mixture, mixing on low speed until just blended; stir in toasted walnuts. Spoon into the prepared muffin pan.

4. Bake for 25 to 30 minutes, until a toothpick inserted in the center comes out clean. Remove and cool on a wire rack. Serve warm or at room temperature.

WILD-BLUEBERRY BRAN MUFFINS

If you're lucky enough to live close to a source of wild blueberries, this is the recipe for you. Blueberries of any kind hold myriad preventive-health powers. However, wild blueberries grow smaller and sweeter than cultivated berries and contain higher levels of beneficial polyphenols (anthocyanins and procyanidins) that are believed to support brain, vascular, and overall health. The bran provides a healthy dose of fiber and texture—pleasing on all counts. **Yields approximately 36 muffins**

INGREDIENTS

3 cups bran cereal

2½ cups buttermilk or sour milk (see page 40)

1½ cups plain yogurt

3 cups all-purpose flour

2½ tablespoons baking powder

1 teaspoon baking soda

½ teaspoon salt

¾ cup wheat germ

3 eggs

¾ cup unsulfured molasses

¾ cup maple syrup

½ cup firmly packed brown sugar

⅓ cup virgin coconut oil, melted

3 cups fresh, wild blueberries

1. Preheat oven to 400°F. Grease one to three standard muffin pans or line with paper cups; set aside.

2. In a large bowl, combine cereal, buttermilk, and yogurt; let stand 15 minutes.

3. In a separate bowl, combine flour, baking powder, baking soda, and salt. Stir in wheat germ.

4. In another bowl, blend eggs, molasses, syrup, brown sugar, and oil; stir into bran mixture and mix well. Add to flour–wheat germ mixture and mix just to moisten. Fold in blueberries.

5. Scoop ¼ cup batter into each muffin cavity and bake for 20 to 25 minutes, until a toothpick inserted in the center comes out clean. Cool on a wire rack for 5 minutes before serving. Serve warm.

WHOLE-GRAIN ASIAN PEAR MUFFINS

No one can argue that Asian pears are a true seasonal treat. Their sweet, crisp flesh and unique flavor is worth the wait each year. This recipe calls for dried Asian pears, which can be found online (look for Harvester Farms brand freeze-dried), or if you're so inclined, try drying some yourself in your dehydrator or oven when they're in season. **Yields 24 muffins**

INGREDIENTS

1 cup rolled oats

1 cup wheat bran

1 cup wheat germ (untoasted)

1 cup boiling water

2 eggs, slightly beaten

2 cups buttermilk or sour milk, room temperature (see page 40)

½ cup virgin coconut oil, melted

1 cup dried Asian pears, chopped

2½ cups all-purpose flour

1 cup sugar

2 teaspoons baking powder

1 teaspoon baking soda

½ teaspoon salt

1 teaspoon apple pie spice

1 teaspoon ground cinnamon

Pinch ground cloves

1. Preheat oven to 350°F. Grease two standard muffin pans or line with paper cups; set aside.

2. In a large bowl, combine rolled oats, wheat bran, and wheat germ. Add boiling water and stir with a fork to moisten evenly; let cool 5 to 10 minutes. Stir in eggs, buttermilk, oil, and dried pears; blend well.

3. In another bowl, stir together flour, sugar, baking powder, baking soda, salt, and spices. Fold into wet mixture and stir lightly until just blended; do not overmix.

4. Muffins can be baked all at once or several at a time. Store extra batter tightly covered for up to 1 week in the refrigerator. Stir before each use.

5. Divide batter evenly into the muffin pans. Bake for 20 minutes, until a toothpick inserted in the center comes out clean. Cool on a wire rack for 5 minutes before turning out.

CARROT-APPLE NUT MUFFINS

Fall means an abundance of bright-orange carrots, sweet apples, and crunchy nuts. You may not think to combine them in a sunny-looking, morning muffin, but this carrot-apple nut muffin recipe does just that—and with delicious results. **Yields 6 jumbo muffins or 12 standard muffins**

INGREDIENTS

2 cups all-purpose flour

1 cup sugar (brown, white, or a combination)

¾ teaspoon baking soda

1½ teaspoons baking powder

½ teaspoon salt

½ teaspoon ground cinnamon

½ cup walnuts or pecans, chopped

3 eggs

¼ cup virgin coconut oil, melted

¼ cup unsalted butter, melted

¼ cup sour cream

½ teaspoon grated fresh ginger

1 teaspoon vanilla extract

2 cups peeled and finely grated carrots (about 2 or 3)

1 large apple, peeled and finely grated

1. Preheat oven to 350°F. Grease a standard or jumbo muffin pan or line with paper cups; set aside.

2. In a large bowl, whisk together the flour, sugar, baking soda, baking powder, salt, and ground cinnamon. Stir in the nuts. Set aside.

3. In a separate bowl, whisk together the eggs, oil, melted butter, sour cream, ginger, and vanilla extract. Fold the wet ingredients and the grated carrot and apple into the flour mixture, stirring just until moistened. Divide the batter evenly into the prepared muffin pan.

4. Bake for 20 to 25 minutes, until a toothpick inserted in the center comes out clean. Cool on a wire rack for 5 minutes before turning out.

TROPICAL APPLESAUCE MUFFINS

We could call this a true Renaissance muffin. It blends the familiar (apples) with the exotic (coconut and pineapple qualify) for a healthy treat that provides a known comfort while satisfying your taste for adventure. **Yields 12 muffins**

INGREDIENTS

1 cup whole wheat flour

1 cup all-purpose flour

⅔ cup sugar

½ teaspoon salt

2 teaspoons baking powder

⅔ cup coconut milk

¼ cup applesauce

½ teaspoon vanilla extract

1 egg, beaten

½ cup chopped pineapple (fresh or canned)

½ cup unsweetened shredded coconut

1. Preheat oven to 400°F. Grease a standard muffin pan or line with paper cups; set aside.

2. In a medium bowl, sift together the flours, sugar, salt, and baking powder. Set aside.

3. In a large bowl, whisk together the coconut milk, applesauce, vanilla, and egg. Stir in the dry ingredients, then fold in the pineapple and coconut. Divide the batter evenly in the muffin pan.

4. Bake for 20 minutes, until a toothpick inserted in the center comes out clean. Cool on a wire rack for 5 minutes before turning out.

ALMOND MUFFINS

A meal's worth of nutrition in a muffin? It's possible with this healthy recipe. Most of these ingredients should be available in the natural-foods section of the grocery store. If you prefer to make almond meal instead of buying it, do this: drop unblanched almonds into the blender, a handful at a time, in the amount you need for a recipe; process until a fine meal develops. As for the choice between rice bran and rice polish, just bear in mind that the polish is lighter, but the bran is more nutritious. **Yields 12 muffins**

INGREDIENTS

½ cup buckwheat flour

½ cup whole wheat flour

½ cup almond meal

½ cup rice bran (or rice polish)

½ cup raw or turbinado sugar

3 teaspoons baking powder

½ teaspoon baking soda

¼ cup unsulfured molasses

¾ cup water or milk

2 eggs, beaten

½ cup raisins (optional)

1. Preheat oven to 350°F. Grease and flour a standard muffin pan or line with paper cups; set aside.

2. In a large bowl, mix together the flours, almond meal, rice bran, sugar, baking powder, and baking soda. In a small bowl, mix together the molasses, water or milk, and eggs.

3. Pour the wet ingredients into the dry ingredients and mix until they're well moistened (do not beat; stir only until the mixture is relatively smooth). Fold in raisins if using. Pour the batter into the prepared muffin pan.

4. Bake for 20 to 30 minutes, until a toothpick inserted in the center comes out clean. Cool for 5 minutes in the pan before turning out onto a wire rack to cool completely.

WHOLE WHEAT MUFFINS

These muffins offer a nice, clean whole wheat flavor with just a hint of sweetness. They are moist and savory—an ideal accompaniment to supper, in place of a dinner roll. Serve warm with whipped honey butter.
Yields 12 muffins

INGREDIENTS

2 cups whole wheat flour

2 teaspoons baking powder

2 tablespoons sugar

1 egg, slightly beaten

1 cup milk

2 tablespoons unsalted butter, melted

2 tablespoons sour cream

1. Preheat oven to 400°F. Grease a standard muffin pan or line with paper cups; set aside.

2. In a large bowl, sift together the flour, baking powder, and sugar.

3. In a separate bowl, combine egg, milk, butter, and sour cream. Add the wet ingredients to the dry ingredients all at once, stirring only enough to moisten. Fill each cavity of the prepared muffin pan two-thirds full.

4. Bake for about 20 minutes, until nicely browned and a toothpick inserted in the center comes out clean. Cool on a wire rack for 5 minutes before serving.

SAVORY BACON MUFFINS

The three Bs—buckwheat, buttermilk, and bacon—make this recipe special. Botanically speaking, buckwheat is not technically a grain at all, but a cousin of the rhubarb plant, so it is suitable for gluten-free baking. The nutrients and nutty flavor of buckwheat have led this "pseudograin" to be accepted into the family of grains. Health benefits include high levels of an antioxidant called rutin, and studies show that it improves circulation and prevents LDL cholesterol from blocking blood vessels. **Yields 12 muffins**

INGREDIENTS

1⅓ cups all-purpose flour

¾ cup buckwheat flour

1½ teaspoons baking powder

½ teaspoon baking soda

¼ teaspoon salt

¼ cup honey

2 eggs, beaten

½ cup buttermilk or sour milk (see page 40)

2 tablespoons unsalted butter, melted

¾ cup sour cream

¼ cup minced onion

¼ cup thinly sliced green onions

½ cup cooked, crumbled bacon

1. Preheat oven to 375°F. Grease a standard muffin pan or line with paper cups; set aside.

2. In a medium bowl, whisk together the flours, baking powder, baking soda, and salt. Make a well in the center and set aside.

3. In a separate bowl, combine honey, eggs, buttermilk, and melted butter. Stir in the sour cream. Add to the flour mixture all at once and stir. Fold in onions and bacon. Divide the batter evenly into the prepared muffin pan.

4. Bake for 20 minutes, until a toothpick inserted in the center comes out clean. Cool on a wire rack for 5 minutes. Serve muffins with butter and honey, if desired.

SUNFLOWER HONEY OAT-BRAN MUFFINS

These muffins are bursting with flavors and textures sure to please. The streusel topping is a nice addition but optional if you are trying to lower your sugar consumption. These muffins make a healthful midday snack or a quick breakfast on the go. **Yields 12 muffins**

INGREDIENTS

1½ cups oat bran

½ cup oat flour

½ cup whole wheat flour

½ cup all-purpose flour

1½ teaspoons baking powder

1½ teaspoons baking soda

¼ teaspoon salt

2 eggs

1 cup milk, room temperature

2 tablespoons virgin coconut oil, melted

2 tablespoons apple-cider vinegar

⅓ cup honey

2 tablespoons unsulfured molasses

½ cup rolled oats

½ cup unsalted shelled sunflower seeds

OPTIONAL TOPPING

1 tablespoon raw or turbinado sugar

1 tablespoon brown sugar

1 tablespoon rolled oats

1 tablespoon unsalted shelled sunflower seeds

1. In a large bowl, stir together the oat bran, flours, baking powder, baking soda, and salt. In a separate large bowl, whisk eggs for about a minute. Whisk in milk, oil, and vinegar. Stir in honey and molasses.

2. Add the dry ingredients to the wet ingredients a little at a time. Stir in the rolled oats and sunflower seeds. Let the batter sit at room temperature for at least 15 minutes.

3. Preheat oven to 375°F. Grease a standard muffin pan or line with paper cups; set aside.

4. Prepare the topping, if using: In a small bowl, stir together the sugars, oats, and sunflower seeds. Set aside.

5. Fill the muffin cups two-thirds full. Divide the topping evenly and sprinkle over each muffin. Bake for 15 to 20 minutes, until a toothpick inserted in the center comes out clean. Turn muffins out onto a wire rack to cool.

ORANGE-CRANBERRY WHEAT GERM MUFFINS

The sweet-tart flavors of orange and cranberry are a real palate pleaser. If you grind your own wheat berries into flour, this will be easy for you; if you don't, use the pastry flour as recommended. Look for unsweetened or apple-juice-sweetened cranberries (instead of sugar-sweetened Craisins) for a healthier muffin. **Yields 24 muffins**

INGREDIENTS

3 cups freshly ground white or whole wheat pastry flour

1 cup wheat germ or bran

2 teaspoons baking powder

1 teaspoon baking soda

1 teaspoon ground cinnamon

½ teaspoon salt

¼ teaspoon ground nutmeg

1 cup firmly packed brown sugar

1 cup dried cranberries

¼ cup unsalted butter, melted

¼ cup applesauce

2 teaspoons orange zest

2 tablespoons orange extract plus enough water to equal 1 cup

4 eggs, beaten

1. Preheat oven to 375°F. Grease two standard muffin pans or line with paper cups; set aside.

2. In a large bowl, whisk together the flour, wheat germ or bran, baking powder, baking soda, cinnamon, salt, nutmeg, and sugar. Stir in the cranberries. Make a well in the center.

3. In another bowl, combine the melted butter, applesauce, orange zest, orange extract with water, and eggs; mix well. Add wet ingredients to dry ingredients and stir until just combined. Spoon batter evenly into muffin cups.

4. Bake for 17 to 20 minutes, until a toothpick inserted in the center comes out clean. Cool for 5 minutes in the pan before turning out onto a wire rack to cool completely.

LEMON POPPY SEED MINI MUFFINS

We love bite-size, pack-portable muffins, especially when they are loaded with lemony, poppy seed flavor. If you don't have a mini-muffin pan, use a regular-size muffin pan for equally good results. For an extra hint of lemon, add a dash of lemon extract to the batter. **Yields 24 mini muffins or 12 standard muffins**

INGREDIENTS

1 large egg

¼ cup virgin coconut oil, melted

⅓ cup sugar

2 tablespoons poppy seeds

1 tablespoon lemon zest

1 tablespoon fresh lemon juice

1 teaspoon vanilla extract

8 ounces (1 cup) plain yogurt

1 teaspoon baking powder

½ teaspoon baking soda

1¾ cups plus 1 tablespoon sifted whole wheat pastry flour or all-purpose flour

1. Preheat oven to 375°F. Grease the muffin pans or line with paper cups; set aside.

2. In a large mixing bowl, beat the egg, oil, sugar, poppy seeds, lemon zest, lemon juice, and vanilla. Mix in the yogurt just until blended. In a separate bowl, stir together the baking powder, baking soda, and flour. Add to the wet ingredients and mix slowly, just until blended. Pour the batter into the muffin pan, filling each cavity three-quarters full.

3. Bake 15 minutes for mini muffins, 20 minutes for regular muffins, until lightly browned. Let cool for 10 minutes before removing them from the pan. If you didn't use paper liners, run a butter knife around the edge of each muffin to loosen. Cool for 5 minutes in the pan before turning out onto a wire rack to cool completely.

CHOCOLATE–CHOCOLATE CHIP MUFFINS

These chocolate muffins hide a blood-red secret that's good for you: beets! From lowering your blood pressure to fighting inflammation, beets are a powerhouse of nutrition and health benefits that just happen to keep baked goods moist. We've replaced much of the sugar with raw agave nectar, and most of the oil with puréed apples, making these muffins a sweet treat you can feel good about. **Yields 12 muffins**

INGREDIENTS

3 medium red beets

2 medium apples, cored and chopped

2 eggs

½ cup evaporated cane juice (or granulated sugar)

½ cup raw agave nectar

4 tablespoons unsalted butter, melted

1 tablespoon vanilla extract

¼ cup water

1 cup all-purpose flour

¾ cup whole wheat pastry flour

½ cup cocoa powder

¼ teaspoon salt

2 teaspoons baking soda

⅓ cup dark (or bittersweet) chocolate chips

1. Preheat oven to 350°F. Grease and flour a standard muffin pan or line with paper cups; set aside.

2. Prepare the veggies and fruits: Scrub the unpeeled beets and boil them whole (cutting off the greens if still attached) in a saucepan until easily pierced by a fork, about 30 to 40 minutes. Put cooked beets into a food processor or blender with the chopped apples and purée until smooth.

3. Prepare the wet mixture: In a large bowl, beat the eggs with the cane juice (or sugar) on high speed until frothy, about 3 to 5 minutes. Mix in the agave nectar, melted butter, vanilla, beet/apple mixture, and water. Mix just until well combined.

4. Prepare the dry mixture: In a large bowl, sift the flours and cocoa. Stir in the salt and baking soda until well mixed. Gradually add the dry ingredients to the wet ingredients and mix until just combined. Stir in chocolate chips.

5. Fill each cavity of the prepared muffin pan two-thirds full with batter. Bake for 20 minutes, until a toothpick in the center comes out clean. Cool for 5 minutes in the pan before turning out onto a wire rack to cool completely.

CHOCOLATE-BACON MUFFINS

These qualify as sweet and savory, and for anyone who scoffs at the notion of a bacon-chocolate pairing, here's our advice: Try it before you knock it! The salty smokiness of bacon marries with the sweetness of chocolate, and a perfect union is formed. **Yields 12 muffins**

INGREDIENTS

6 slices bacon

1¾ cups all-purpose flour

½ cup plus 2 tablespoons firmly packed brown sugar

¼ cup cocoa powder

1 teaspoon baking powder

1 teaspoon baking soda

¼ teaspoon salt

1 cup warm water

¼ cup unsalted butter, melted

1 tablespoon strong coffee

1 teaspoon vanilla extract

1 egg

¾ cup mini semisweet chocolate chips, divided

1. Preheat oven to 400°F. Grease and flour a standard muffin pan or line with paper cups; set aside.

2. Fry bacon until cooked but not yet crispy. Transfer to a paper-towel-lined plate. Once cool, chop into ¼-inch pieces; set aside.

3. In a large mixing bowl, combine flour, sugar, cocoa, baking powder, baking soda, and salt. Whisk together.

4. In a separate bowl, combine water, butter, coffee, vanilla, and egg; stir together. Stir in ½ cup chocolate chips and half the bacon. Add to the flour mixture and stir just until moist.

5. Divide batter evenly among 12 cups. Sprinkle remaining ¼ cup chocolate chips and remaining bacon evenly over batter.

6. Bake for 15 minutes, until a toothpick inserted in the center comes out clean. Cool for 5 minutes before turning out. Store leftovers in refrigerator.

HUCKLEBERRY AND HONEY SCONES

The huckleberry is a small, round, bluish-black berry that's related to the blueberry—it's the state fruit of Idaho and grows mainly in the West. Some varieties taste very similar to blueberries, while others are much tarter or sweeter. In lieu of fresh huckleberries, you can simply substitute blueberries in this recipe. **Yields 8 scones**

INGREDIENTS

2½ cups unbleached all-purpose flour, divided

¾ cup fresh huckleberries, rinsed and dried

1 tablespoon baking powder

6 tablespoons unsalted butter, chilled and cubed

¼ cup honey

¾ cup half-and-half

1 egg

1. Preheat oven to 350°F. Line a baking sheet with parchment paper and set aside.

2. In a small bowl, combine ½ cup of the flour with the huckleberries; toss to coat. In a large bowl, mix remaining 2 cups of flour with baking powder. Using a pastry blender or two knives, cut in butter until the mixture resembles coarse meal.

3. In another bowl, beat together the honey, half-and-half, and egg. Add to dry ingredients. Gently stir in huckleberries.

4. Turn dough onto a lightly floured work surface and knead a few times. Form into a ball, then roll out to a 10-inch circle, about 1 inch thick. Cut into 8 sections. Place on prepared baking sheet.

5. Bake for 10 minutes, until golden brown.

RASPBERRY SCONES

When you're ready for a tea treat—something sweet yet healthy—bake a batch of these scones, plop them into resealable plastic freezer bags, and store them in the back of the freezer for those desperate moments when you need one.

Instead of using a rolling pin and biscuit cutter, drop these scones onto a baking sheet; it's much faster. Serve warm with butter or yogurt cheese and raspberry jam. **Yields 18 scones**

INGREDIENTS

2 cups sifted whole wheat pastry flour or unbleached all-purpose flour

½ teaspoon baking powder

½ teaspoon baking soda

¼ teaspoon ground nutmeg

2 tablespoons sugar

¼ cup old-fashioned rolled oats

3 tablespoons unsalted butter, chilled and cubed

2 tablespoons honey

½ teaspoon almond extract

½ cup buttermilk or sour milk (see page 40)

1 cup frozen raspberries* (keep frozen until ready to use)

*The berries need to be frost-free—without excess ice crystals—or the scones will be mushy.

1. Preheat oven to 375°F. Grease a large baking sheet; set aside.

2. Measure the flour, baking powder, baking soda, nutmeg, sugar, and oats into a large bowl or the bowl of a food processor. Add the butter and pulse the processor a few times until the dough looks like coarse meal. (If you are not using a food processor, use a pastry blender or two knives to cut in the butter.)

3. Add the honey, almond extract, and buttermilk and pulse just until blended. Briefly pulse in the frozen berries; overmixing will crush them. Using a small (2-tablespoon) ice cream scoop, scoop the batter onto the baking sheet in balls at least 1 inch apart. They should be about 1½ inches in diameter and about 1 inch high.

4. Bake for 20 minutes, until lightly browned. Cool a few minutes; remove with a spatula. Serve warm.

WILD-BLACKBERRY SCONES

Wild blackberries, unlike their cultivated counterparts, tend to be smaller and seedier but are equally sweet if picked at their peak. Pick them from brambles in the evening, just before sunset, to collect all the berries that have ripened during the day but before the local wildlife gets them. Wild-blackberry bushes are thick and sprawling, but they bear remarkably few berries for the thicket of vegetation. For this reason, we like this scone recipe because only a handful of fresh berries is required, and it comes together in a flash. **Yields 6 scones**

INGREDIENTS

1 cup whole wheat flour

1 cup unbleached all-purpose flour

1 tablespoon baking powder

¼ cup granulated sugar

½ teaspoon salt

6 tablespoons unsalted butter, chilled and cubed

1 cup wild blackberries

¾ cup sour cream

⅓ cup milk

Raw or turbinado sugar, for sprinkling

1. Preheat oven to 425°F. Line a baking sheet with parchment paper.

2. In a large bowl, whisk together the flours, baking powder, sugar, and salt.

3. Using a pastry blender or two knives, cut in the butter until the mixture resembles coarse meal. Toss in the blackberries and break them into chunks with the pastry blender. Add the sour cream and milk, mixing with a rubber spatula until the dough comes together.

4. Using your hands, bring the dough together in a ball and turn it out onto a floured work surface. Pat the dough into a 1-inch-high disk and divide it into 6 even wedges with a sharp knife. Transfer the scones to the baking sheet and sprinkle with turbinado sugar.

5. Bake the scones for approximately 15 minutes, until golden around the edges. Let cool for a minute and then transfer to a wire rack.

MAPLE SCONES WITH LEMON VERBENA

You can use any lemon herb that you like in these scones; orange mint is also delicious. Of course, using fresh herbs will give you the most wonderful bouquet in addition to flavor. However, you may use dried herbs if need be—reduce the amount of dried herbs to about 2 tablespoons, stir into the milk, and let stand for about 10 to 15 minutes. The scones can be prepared with all unbleached flour, which will make them a bit lighter; the whole wheat flour makes them a bit more hearty. **Yields 8 to 12 scones**

INGREDIENTS

2 cups unbleached all-purpose flour

½ cup whole wheat flour

¾ teaspoon salt

3 teaspoons baking powder

8 tablespoons unsalted butter, chilled and cut into small pieces

¼ cup chopped candied ginger

¾ cup milk

¼ cup plus 1 tablespoon pure maple syrup

About 4 tablespoons freshly chopped lemon verbena

1. Preheat oven to 425°F.

2. In a large bowl, combine flours, salt, and baking powder and blend thoroughly. Using a pastry blender or two knives, cut in butter until mixture resembles coarse meal. Stir in candied ginger.

3. In a small bowl, stir together the milk, ¼ cup of maple syrup, and lemon verbena. Add liquid to dry ingredients and stir to form a soft dough.

4. Turn the dough onto a floured work surface or silicone mat; knead gently with a few turns, until it just comes together. Roll dough out into a circular shape, about ¾ inch thick. Brush the top of the dough with remaining maple syrup. Cut dough into 8 or 12 wedges with a sharp knife or pizza cutter and place on an ungreased baking sheet.

5. Bake scones for 18 to 20 minutes, until golden brown. Remove to a wire rack to cool slightly before serving. The scones are best served warm and right after baking. If you want to prepare them in advance, cool them completely and store them in an airtight container. Wrap them in foil and gently reheat at 325°F for 10 to 15 minutes.

CHOCOLATE CHIP SCONES

These chocolaty scones are delicious on their own, but if you want to try some variations, substitute half-and-half or light cream for the milk; add ¼ cup finely chopped toasted pecans or walnuts, or 2 to 3 teaspoons freshly grated orange peel to the dry ingredients. Before baking, brush tops lightly with milk or cream and sprinkle with sugar. They're best eaten warm when the chocolate is a little melty. Serve with butter or crème fraîche and your favorite preserves. **Yields 12 scones**

INGREDIENTS

3½ cups unbleached all-purpose
   flour

½ cup sugar

2 teaspoons baking powder

½ teaspoon salt

¾ cup unsalted butter, chilled
   and cut into small pieces

¼ cup mini chocolate chips

4 eggs

½ cup milk

1. Preheat oven to 425°F. Grease a baking sheet; set aside.

2. In a large bowl, combine flour, sugar, baking powder, and salt. Using a pastry blender or two knives, cut in butter until the mixture resembles coarse meal. Add chocolate chips; toss to mix.

3. In a medium bowl, beat eggs and milk until blended. Stir into the flour mixture with a fork just until dry ingredients are moistened.

4. Turn dough onto a lightly floured work surface and knead for a few strokes; pat to ¾ inch thick. Cut dough into rounds with a lightly floured 3-inch cutter; place on the prepared baking sheet. Gather up the scraps and repeat to use up all the dough.

5. Bake for 10 minutes, until golden brown. Cool on a wire rack.

SAVORY SAGE SCONES

Sage is the herb that makes chicken soup sing. It adds robust flavor to focaccia, homemade bread sticks, or quick breads such as biscuits or scones. Or you can mix it into a soft cheese for a tasty spread. Use a light hand with sage, whether fresh or dried, because a little goes a long way.

If you don't grow sage and must purchase it, you'll need to choose between fresh, rubbed, or ground. Use fresh sage whenever possible, and dry extra leaves to store whole. For the freshest taste, crumble or rub dried sage leaves between your fingers or the palms of your hands just before adding them to foods. Buy rubbed sage rather than ground sage, which usually tastes somewhat bitter and has a shorter shelf life than the other kinds.

Yields 8 scones

INGREDIENTS

½ cup whole wheat flour

1½ cups unbleached all-purpose flour

1 teaspoon baking powder

1 teaspoon salt

1 teaspoon sugar

¼ teaspoon black pepper

2 tablespoons chopped fresh sage (or 1 tablespoon dried)

1 teaspoon chopped fresh thyme (or ½ teaspoon dried)

1 cup grated sharp cheddar cheese

1 egg

3 tablespoons olive oil

¾ cup buttermilk or sour milk (see page 40)

8 whole sage leaves

1. Preheat oven to 425°F. Grease a baking sheet or use a baking stone. Do not preheat.

2. In a large bowl, mix together the flours, baking powder, salt, sugar, pepper, sage, and thyme. Stir in the cheese.

3. In a separate bowl, beat the egg with the oil and buttermilk (or milk), and add to the flour mixture all at once. Stir until dry ingredients are just moistened, about 15 strokes.

4. Using floured hands, lightly knead the dough 4 or 5 times in the bowl. Transfer dough to the prepared baking sheet or baking stone. Shape it into an 8-inch-wide circle. Using a sharp knife, cut the circle into 8 wedges, but do not separate them. Lightly press one sage leaf onto the top of each wedge.

5. Bake 18 to 20 minutes, until lightly browned. Transfer to a wire rack to cool. Serve warm with butter and honey.

Biscuits & Cornbread

· ·

What is the secret to making "perfect" biscuits? Making a lot of lousy biscuits, of course! Seriously, to get the knack for making biscuits, you just have to do it over and over again. You'll make several batches of really terrible biscuits; then you'll graduate to lots of mediocre biscuits; eventually, you'll get the hang of it, and your biscuits will be decent. Keep at it for several years and then you will make superb biscuits.

That said, there's no reason not to start off on the right foot. Here are our secrets for "perfect" biscuits:

1. Use real, full-fat buttermilk. If you can produce or find it, use the real deal. It gives the biscuits a wonderfully tender texture and helps the leaveners rise better.

2. Use real butter or lard. Biscuits just aren't the same without real butter or home-rendered lard from pastured hogs. Shortening or margarine can do in a pinch, but real fats are the way to go for excellent biscuits.

3. Use a pastry blender. This little gadget cuts the fat into the dry ingredients quickly and easily. You can use a fork or two knives or a food processor set on "pulse," but a pastry blender is definitely worth the few dollars you'll pay for it if you plan on making lots of biscuits.

4. Cook in a cast-iron skillet. There's nothing like the texture of a homemade biscuit baked in a cast-iron pan. The outside of the biscuit will be slightly crusty, and the insides will be steamy-soft and flaky.

5. Be gentle. Biscuit dough needs a gentle touch. Save the pounding for yeast doughs. Light handling of biscuit dough yields a soft, delicate biscuit. Pour in the wet ingredients and gently stir the dough just until blended. Don't overmix it. You'll ruin your biscuits.

GRANDMA'S HOMEMADE BISCUITS

These biscuits are as authentic as they come, from a time when lard from the family's hog and milk from the backyard cow were common fare. The dough can be rolled and cut with a biscuit cutter, or dropped by the wooden spoonful. Make these for a big family supper, as biscuits are best when eaten fresh from the oven.
Yields 12 biscuits

INGREDIENTS

2½ cups unbleached all-purpose flour, divided

3 teaspoons baking powder

½ teaspoon salt

⅓ cup plus 1 tablespoon chilled lard, coarsely chopped

1 cup milk

1 tablespoon salted butter, melted (optional)

1. Preheat oven to 400°F. Grease a baking sheet; set aside.

2. Place 2 cups of flour, the baking powder, and the salt in a large mixing bowl; whisk together.

3. Using a pastry blender or two knives, work the lard into the flour mixture until it resembles coarse meal. Add the milk and stir.

4. On a silicone mat or work surface, sprinkle the remaining ½ cup of flour. Turn out the dough mixture and knead for a few minutes. Roll out the dough to 1 inch thick and cut with a biscuit cutter; alternatively, drop the dough using a large spoon and pat down onto the prepared baking sheet spaced 1 inch apart. For color, brush the biscuits with melted butter, if desired.

5. Bake for 20 minutes, until the tops are golden brown.

BUTTERMILK BISCUITS

These classic buttermilk biscuits are the gold standard: a little tart and rich, but very tender. You can make the dough ahead of time, and it will keep for several weeks in the refrigerator—perfect for the holidays when you may not have time to make *everything* from scratch. **Yields 24 biscuits**

INGREDIENTS

5 cups unbleached all-purpose flour

1 teaspoon baking powder

1 teaspoon baking soda

1 teaspoon salt

3 tablespoons sugar

¾ cup lard or unsalted butter, chilled and cubed

4½ teaspoons active dry yeast

½ cup warm water

2 cups buttermilk or sour milk (see page 40)

1. Preheat oven to 450°F.

2. In a large bowl sift together the flour, baking powder, baking soda, salt, and sugar. Using a pastry blender or two knives, cut in the lard or butter until mixture resembles coarse meal.

3. Dissolve the yeast in the water. Add buttermilk and yeast mixture to flour mixture. Mix with a spoon until moist. Cover and refrigerate until ready to use.

4. To use, generously flour a work surface. Roll out dough to ½ to ¾ inch thick. Cut biscuits with the rim of drinking glass or a biscuit cutter and transfer to a greased baking sheet, placing 1 inch apart. Gather up the scraps and repeat to use up all the dough.

5. Bake for 12 minutes, until tops are golden brown.

WHOLE WHEAT BISCUITS

These morsels made from half white flour and half whole wheat flour are denser than biscuits made with all-white flour, but the taste is superb, especially when made with freshly ground wheat berries. Lard will give superior texture, so don't shy away from this healthy fat. **Yields 10 to 16 biscuits**

INGREDIENTS

1 cup whole wheat flour

1 cup unbleached all-purpose flour

1 tablespoon baking powder

¼ cup lard or unsalted butter, chilled and cubed

¾ cup milk

1. Preheat oven to 450°F.

2. In a large bowl, whisk together the flours and baking powder. Using a pastry blender or two knives, cut in the lard or butter until mixture resembles coarse meal. Stir in enough milk to make a soft dough that leaves the sides of the bowl and sticks to the mixing fork.

3. Turn dough onto a lightly floured work surface and knead 15 times. Roll out to ½ inch thick. Cut with a 2-inch biscuit cutter (or the rim of a drinking glass dipped in flour) or into rectangles and place on an ungreased baking sheet. For soft sides, place close together; for crusty sides, place 1 inch apart. Gather up the scraps and repeat to use up all the dough.

4. Bake for 10 to 12 minutes, until golden brown. Serve at once.

BAKING POWDER BISCUITS

Buttermilk biscuits typically require a combination of baking powder and baking soda to achieve the proper acid-base balance for optimal leavening. Since these biscuits are made without buttermilk, we left out the soda (a base) and relied solely on baking powder. They are buttery, fluffy, and delicious and are just the thing for a breakfast of biscuits and gravy. **Yields 8 biscuits**

INGREDIENTS

2 cups unbleached all-purpose flour

2 teaspoons baking powder

1½ teaspoons salt

2 teaspoons sugar

8 tablespoons unsalted butter, cut into ½-inch pieces and frozen for 10 to 30 minutes, plus 1 to 2 tablespoons melted, for brushing the tops of the biscuits

1 to 1¼ cups milk

1. Preheat oven to 450°F. Line a baking sheet with parchment paper. Place another large piece of parchment paper on the counter for shaping and wrapping the dough, and sprinkle very lightly with flour.

2. In a large mixing bowl, whisk together the flour, baking powder, salt, and sugar. Use a pastry blender (or two knives, forks, or a food processor) to cut in the butter, repeatedly pressing or slicing the butter into the flour until the largest slivers or chunks of butter are no larger than very small peas.

3. Slowly pour one cup of milk into the flour mixture and use a wooden spoon or rubber spatula to gently incorporate, just until the dough comes together, adding the remaining ¼ cup of milk only as needed. The dough should not be wet or overly sticky. It should be a little scrappy looking.

4. Turn the dough out onto the prepared parchment paper. Lightly flour your hands and use them to gently pat the dough into a 1-inch-thick rectangle, approximately 8 x 6 inches. Gently wrap up the dough in the parchment and freeze for 5 to 10 minutes.

5. Use a sharp pizza cutter to cut the chilled dough into 8 (approximately 2 x 3 inch) rectangles, or use a biscuit cutter to make circles, if desired. Place the biscuits on the prepared baking sheet; brush the tops gently with half the melted butter.

6. Bake for 15 minutes, until puffed up and lightly golden. Gently brush the tops with the remaining butter and serve with butter and jam or honey.

7. Leftover biscuits may be cooled completely and stored in a resealable plastic bag or well-sealed container at room temperature for up to 2 days. Reheat leftover biscuits in a 350°F oven for 5 minutes for best results.

CHIVE AND PARMESAN BISCUITS

These cheesy bites are delicious when made with buttermilk, but if you don't have any on hand, place 1 tablespoon lemon juice or vinegar in a measuring cup. Add enough milk to make 1 cup. Stir and let stand for 5 minutes before using.

If you want to prepare these biscuits in advance of a special occasion, cool them completely and store them in an airtight container. Wrap in foil and gently reheat at 325°F for 10 to 15 minutes. **Yields 12 biscuits**

INGREDIENTS

2 cups unbleached all-purpose flour

Scant ½ teaspoon salt

1½ teaspoons baking powder

½ teaspoon baking soda

Pinch cayenne pepper

¼ teaspoon paprika

½ cup freshly grated Parmesan cheese

5 tablespoons unsalted butter

1 cup buttermilk or sour milk (see page 40)

½ cup snipped chives

1. Preheat oven to 400°F.

2. In a large bowl, combine flour, salt, baking powder, baking soda, cayenne, paprika, and Parmesan and blend thoroughly. Using a pastry blender or two knives, cut in butter until mixture resembles coarse meal.

3. In a small bowl, combine buttermilk with chives. Add liquid to dry ingredients and stir to form a soft dough. Turn dough onto a floured work surface and knead gently until it just comes together. Roll out to not quite ½ inch thick. Cut dough into 2½-inch rounds with biscuit cutter or the rim of a drinking glass and place on an ungreased baking sheet. Gather up the scraps and repeat to use up all the dough.

4. Bake for 18 to 20 minutes, until light golden brown. Cool for a few minutes before serving.

CAMPFIRE DUTCH OVEN BISCUITS

Cooking over a campfire, when done right, can be an all-day affair—and why shouldn't it be? Build a roaring fire, keep it fed with cured hardwood all day, and let the good times roll as you use that fire to prepare a variety of dishes from beans to these biscuits. Set up a camp table near the fire and let your family and friends help with the preparations. You'll be amazed at the fireside revelations as you dine under the stars and gaze into the flames, and no doubt everyone will leave asking when the next campfire will be. **Yields 3 dozen biscuits**

INGREDIENTS

4 tablespoons plus 1½ teaspoons active dry yeast

½ cup warm water

½ cup honey

¼ cup peanut oil

2 cups buttermilk or sour milk (see page 40)

5 cups unbleached all-purpose flour

½ teaspoon baking soda

4 teaspoons baking powder

1 teaspoon salt

Butter, lard, or cooking spray, for greasing the pan and topping the biscuits

1. In a medium bowl, combine yeast and warm water; let stand for 10 minutes.

2. Stir in honey, oil, and buttermilk.

3. In a large bowl, combine flour, baking soda, baking powder, and salt. Add wet ingredients and stir together to form ball. Turn out onto a floured work surface and knead lightly for 2 minutes.

4. Roll dough to ½ inch thick and cut into 2-inch-round biscuits.

5. Place a 2- or 3-inch-deep cast-iron skillet with lid, or dutch oven with lid, in the fire separately until they're hot but not red. Grease the bottom of the skillet or oven with lard, butter, or cooking spray, and sprinkle with a little flour. Place biscuits inside, touching, and brush the tops with lard, butter, or oil. Cover.

6. Rake out a thin bed of coals and set the skillet or oven on coals. Cover lid with a thick layer of coals.

7. Bake in the fire for 10 to 15 minutes, checking for doneness after 7 minutes.

Tip: Refrigerate unused dough; biscuits can alternatively be baked, uncovered, in a conventional oven at 450°F for 12 to 15 minutes.

BREAKFAST BISCUITS WITH CINNAMON

When you want to put on a special breakfast, like a holiday brunch, make these cinnamon biscuits. Served with apple or honey butter, they are a special treat with their citrusy-sweet glaze. The kids will love these.
Yields 12 biscuits

INGREDIENTS

1¾ cups unbleached all-purpose flour

¼ cup wheat bran

2 tablespoons granulated sugar

1 tablespoon baking powder

½ teaspoon ground cinnamon

¼ teaspoon salt

½ cup butter or lard

⅔ cup milk

½ cup mixed dried fruit bits

½ cup sifted powdered sugar

2 to 3 tablespoons orange juice, milk, or water

1. Preheat oven to 400°F.

2. Combine flour, bran, sugar, baking powder, cinnamon, and salt. Using a pastry blender or two knives, cut in the butter or lard until mixture resembles coarse meal. Make a well in the center of the dry mixture. Add milk and fruit bits; stir just until moistened.

3. Turn dough out onto a floured work surface or silicone mat. Quickly knead the dough 10 to 12 strokes, or until nearly smooth. Pat or lightly roll the dough to ½ inch thick. Cut dough with a floured 2½-inch biscuit cutter or the rim of a drinking glass. Place biscuits 1 inch apart on ungreased baking sheet. Gather up the scraps and repeat to use up all the dough.

4. Bake for 10 to 12 minutes, until golden. Cool for a few minutes on a wire rack.

5. Meanwhile, stir together powdered sugar and enough orange juice to make icing easy to drizzle. Drizzle icing over biscuits; serve warm.

SWEET POTATO BISCUITS

Loaded with potassium, vitamin C, and vitamin A, sweet potatoes are not just healthy but extremely tasty. The most basic way to prepare sweet potatoes is to scrub the skins clean, then prick with a fork and roast in a 400°F oven until soft, around 30 to 40 minutes. Alternatively, you can boil either whole or roughly cut sweet potatoes until fork tender, then purée to use in this recipe. **Yields 20 biscuits**

INGREDIENTS

2 cups whole wheat pastry flour

1½ tablespoons baking powder

½ teaspoon salt

4 tablespoons unsalted butter, chilled

1 cup buttermilk or sour milk (see page 40)

1 cup mashed or puréed sweet potatoes

1 tablespoon honey

1. Preheat oven to 425°F. Grease a baking sheet; set aside.

2. Sift the flour, baking powder, and salt into a medium bowl. Using a pastry blender or two knives, cut the butter into the flour mixture until the mixture looks like coarse meal.

3. In a separate bowl, mix together the milk, sweet potatoes, and honey. Pour into the flour mixture and stir with a fork until the mixture just comes together. Turn the dough out onto a floured work surface and knead, using a light touch, until the dough is fairly smooth. Use a little more flour if the dough is too sticky; a short and gentle kneading will give you the most tender biscuit. Pat the dough out to ¾ to 1 inch thick. Cut with a 2-inch biscuit cutter or the rim of a drinking glass and transfer to the prepared baking sheet. Gather up the scraps and repeat to use up all the dough.

4. Bake for 15 minutes, until just golden. Serve hot.

OLD-FASHIONED CORNBREAD

No chili dinner is complete without a side of cornbread right out of the skillet. It's crispy around the edges, moist enough to eat alone, yet dry enough to soak up soup or chili. Leftovers are good the next day, especially as an old-fashioned breakfast—crumbled up and covered with milk. **Yields 8 servings**

INGREDIENTS

4 cups fine cornmeal

2 teaspoons baking soda

2 teaspoons salt

4 eggs, beaten

4 cups buttermilk or sour milk
(see page 40)

½ cup bacon drippings

1. Preheat oven to 400ºF. Grease a 10-inch cast-iron skillet; set aside.

2. In a large mixing bowl, combine the cornmeal, baking soda, and salt. Add the eggs and buttermilk; mix well. Stir in the bacon drippings. Place the skillet in the hot oven and heat for 3 minutes.

3. Pour batter into the hot skillet and bake for 40 minutes, until golden brown and a toothpick inserted in the center comes out clean.

4. Transfer cornbread to a wire rack immediately by sliding it out with a spatula. Cool for 5 to 10 minutes before cutting and serving.

SWEET BUTTERMILK CORNBREAD

This old-fashioned recipe was written for a crowd, perhaps for a harvesting crew or a hog-butchering contingent. Use buttermilk or sour milk to make an incredibly moist cornbread. **Yields 3 loaves**

INGREDIENTS

5 cups fine cornmeal

2 cups all-purpose flour

¾ teaspoon salt

4 teaspoons baking soda

2 cups firmly packed brown sugar

1 cup lard or unsalted butter, softened

5 eggs

3 cups buttermilk or sour milk
(see page 40)

1. Preheat oven to 350°F. Grease three 9 x 5-inch loaf pans; set aside.

2. In a large bowl, combine cornmeal, flour, salt, and baking soda. In a separate large bowl, cream the brown sugar and lard or butter for 3 minutes on medium-high speed; add eggs and beat well to combine.

3. Alternately add dry ingredients and buttermilk to the creamed mixture, beating well after each addition.

4. Pour the batter evenly into the three prepared pans. Bake for 45 to 60 minutes, until golden brown and a toothpick inserted in the center comes out clean. Allow bread to cool in pans completely before turning out and slicing.

WHOLE-GRAIN CORNBREAD

Whole-grain cornbread can be the ultimate comfort food, and, with all that whole-grain flavor and texture, it offers a different note than recipes that call for highly processed flours and meals. The extra step of preheating the oil in the skillet produces a "fried" bottom crust with a delightful mouthfeel. **Yields 8 servings**

INGREDIENTS

½ cup peanut oil, divided

2 eggs, beaten

1¼ cups half-and-half

1 cup whole wheat flour

1 cup fine whole-grain cornmeal (preferably freshly ground)

2 tablespoons sugar

½ teaspoon salt

2 teaspoons baking powder

1. Place ¼ cup peanut oil in a 10-inch cast-iron skillet and place in the oven. Preheat the oven and skillet to 400°F.

2. In a small bowl, whisk together the eggs, half-and-half, and remaining ¼ cup peanut oil; set aside.

3. In a large bowl, whisk together the flour, cornmeal, sugar, salt, and baking powder. Add the wet ingredients to the dry and stir just until wet.

4. Remove the heated skillet from the oven and pour the batter into it; the oil will sizzle. Bake for 20 to 25 minutes, until golden brown and a toothpick inserted in the center comes out clean. Immediately remove the cornbread from the skillet (it should slide right out with the help of a spatula) and cool on a wire rack. Transfer to a plate to serve. Serve warm with butter and honey.

SKILLET CHEDDAR CORNBREAD

This savory cornbread is rich, cake-like, and full of flavor; the addition of cheese, sage, corn, and chilies makes it a perfect side dish for any Southwestern-style meal, baked beans, or coleslaw. Taste your sage to see how strong it is; if you use a strong-flavored variety like Berggarten, use only about 3 tablespoons. Oregano and marjoram are also very tasty used in place of the sage. **Yields 8 servings**

INGREDIENTS

1 cup all-purpose flour

¼ cup whole wheat flour

1 cup stone-ground cornmeal

2½ teaspoons baking powder

1 teaspoon salt

1 teaspoon chili powder

1 cup milk

3 eggs

¼ cup peanut oil

2 tablespoons honey or sorghum

4 tablespoons finely shredded fresh sage or 1½ tablespoons crumbled dried sage

2 cloves garlic, minced

½ cup finely sliced green onions or chopped yellow onion

2 or 3 serrano or jalapeño peppers, stemmed, seeded, and finely minced

1 cup fresh or thawed frozen corn kernels

1 cup grated sharp cheddar cheese

1. Preheat oven to 375°F. Grease a 10-inch cast-iron skillet.

2. In a large bowl, combine flours, cornmeal, baking powder, salt, and chili powder; blend well.

3. In another bowl, combine milk, eggs, oil, and honey or sorghum; whisk for 1 minute. Stir in the sage, garlic, onions, peppers, and corn.

4. Add the liquid ingredients to the dry ingredients along with the cheese and stir until just mixed. Pour batter into the oiled skillet.

5. Bake for 35 to 40 minutes, until a toothpick inserted in the center comes out clean. Transfer cornbread to a wire rack immediately by sliding it out with a spatula. Cool for 5 to 10 minutes before cutting and serving.

SAVORY BACON, SAGE, AND PEPPERED CORNBREAD

Perhaps cornbread's greatest attribute is its flexibility. Just about any ingredient—sweet or savory—can be added to a basic recipe, and you have a delicious masterpiece on your hands. This cornbread is a great example. The combination of savory and sweet flavors creates something new and different. **Yields 8 servings**

INGREDIENTS

6 slices bacon

1¼ cups cornmeal

¾ cup all-purpose flour

½ teaspoon salt

3 teaspoons baking powder

½ teaspoon hot red pepper flakes

¼ teaspoon ground white pepper

1 teaspoon paprika

1¼ cups buttermilk or sour milk (see page 40)

1 egg

2 tablespoons unsulfured molasses or honey

3 tablespoons chopped fresh sage

2 tablespoons chopped green onions

2 tablespoons freshly grated Parmesan cheese

1. Preheat oven to 425°F.

2. In a 10-inch cast-iron skillet, fry bacon until crisp; reserve fat. Crumble bacon; set aside.

3. In a medium bowl, mix cornmeal, flour, salt, baking powder, pepper flakes, white pepper, and paprika; blend with a fork.

4. In a small bowl, mix buttermilk, egg, and molasses or honey. Pour into dry ingredients. Add chopped sage, green onions, Parmesan cheese, and crumbled bacon; stir well to combine.

5. In the skillet, heat ¼ cup of reserved bacon fat to near smoking, then pour into the batter and stir well. Immediately pour the batter into the hot, greased skillet and bake for 20 to 25 minutes, until golden brown on top and a toothpick inserted in the center comes out clean.

6. Transfer cornbread to a wire rack immediately by sliding it out with a spatula. Cool for 5 to 10 minutes before cutting and serving.

JALAPEÑO CORNBREAD

If plain old cornbread is a family favorite, try this spicy "dressed-up" version to delight and surprise them. Filled with chunks of corn and jalapeños and topped with melted cheese, this side dish is almost a meal in itself. It's versatile enough to serve with a bowl of spicy chili on a cold day or a crisp garden salad on a hot one. For a bit of sweetness to temper the heat of the jalapeños, serve with honey butter. **Yields 9 servings**

INGREDIENTS

1 cup fine cornmeal

1 teaspoon salt

1 teaspoon sugar

3 teaspoons baking powder

⅔ cup buttermilk or sour milk (see page 40)

2 eggs, beaten

½ cup lard or unsalted butter, melted and cooled slightly, plus more for greasing

1 (8.5-ounce) can cream-style corn

1 (4-ounce) can chopped jalapeños, drained

1 cup grated cheddar cheese, divided

1. Preheat oven to 350°F. Grease an 8 x 8-inch glass baking dish with lard or butter; set aside.

2. In a large bowl, combine the cornmeal, salt, sugar, and baking powder and whisk together. Stir in the buttermilk, eggs, lard or butter, and corn and mix well; the batter will be thin.

3. Pour half the batter into the prepared pan. Distribute the jalapeños evenly over the batter and cover with half the cheese. Pour the rest of the batter on top and sprinkle with the remaining cheese.

4. Bake for 30 minutes, until golden brown and a toothpick inserted in the center comes out clean. Cool for 10 minutes before turning it out and slicing.

SWEET CORNBREAD WITH HONEY

If you like your cornbread a little bit sweet, you'll love this basic recipe that uses honey instead of refined sugar. Half flour and half cornmeal produce a lighter bread that pleases adults and kids alike. **Yields 9 servings**

INGREDIENTS

1 cup cornmeal

1 cup all-purpose flour

2 teaspoons baking powder

1 teaspoon baking soda

1 teaspoon salt

1 cup milk

¼ cup honey

2 tablespoons unsalted butter, melted

1 egg

1. Preheat oven to 350°F. Generously grease a 9 x 9-inch baking pan; set aside.

2. In a large bowl, combine cornmeal, flour, baking powder, baking soda, and salt.

3. In a small bowl, whisk together milk, honey, melted butter, and egg.

4. Pour wet ingredients into dry ingredients and mix until just combined. Spoon batter into the prepared pan.

5. Bake for 30 minutes, until golden brown and a toothpick inserted in the center comes out clean. Cool for 10 minutes before turning it out and slicing. Serve warm with butter and honey.

Boiled Breads: Bagels, Pretzels & Dumplings

Just when you thought you had a handle on bread making, here come boiled breads sure to challenge you. Bagels and pretzels involve rolling and shaping, followed by boiling and baking, while dumplings just get boiled and may give you a bit of an easier time.

So what is with boiling? Why do it at all? Well, boiling is responsible for these breads' unique qualities. Specifically, boiling serves three purposes: First, it sets the shape and kills off some of the yeast on the outer surface of the dough, limiting the bagel's or pretzel's expansion when it's later baked. Second, it gelatinizes the starches on the surface, leading to a shiny coating and a chewy texture. Finally, boiling activates the yeast in the inner layers of dough. Once you've baked your way through this chapter, pat yourself on the back and enjoy the confidence of a well-rounded bread maker.

PLAIN BAGELS

For a special treat, forgo the local bakery or grocery store and make your own homemade bagels. Good boiled breads, such as these bagels, are soft and chewy, and they take a while to eat. Fresh from the oven, they're shiny and deliciously yeasty. Create uniquely flavored bagels by following this plain recipe and add your favorite herbs, vegetables, dried fruit, or spices to the dough. **Yields 8 pieces**

INGREDIENTS

4½ cups bread flour, divided

4 teaspoons active dry yeast

1½ cups warm water

1 tablespoon sugar

1½ teaspoons salt

1 egg, for egg wash (optional)

WATER BATH

1 gallon water

1 tablespoon sugar

1. In a large bowl, combine 2 cups of flour and yeast.

2. In a separate bowl, combine warm water, sugar, and salt; combine with flour mixture.

3. In a stand mixer with the paddle attachment, beat at low speed for about 30 seconds, scraping the sides of the bowl; beat an additional 3 minutes on high speed. Incorporate as much of the remaining flour as possible.

4. Turn out dough onto a lightly floured work surface. Knead in additional flour to make a moderately stiff dough. Knead until smooth and elastic. Cover with plastic wrap or a lint-free cotton or linen tea towel (terry cloth will stick and leave lint on the dough) and allow to rest for 15 minutes.

5. Divide the dough into 8 equal portions and roll into balls. Punch a hole in the middle with a floured finger and gently pull to enlarge the hole to 2 inches.

6. Place bagels on a greased baking sheet; cover with a lint-free cotton or linen tea towel and allow to rise for 20 minutes.

7. Meanwhile, heat oven to broil. Prepare the water bath and put it on to boil.

8. After bagels have risen for 20 minutes, broil for 1½ minutes on each side. Reduce oven to 400°F.

9. Once the water bath is boiling, reduce heat. Place bagels, 3 at a time, in water for 1½ minutes, turning after 45 seconds. Drain and place on greased baking sheet. If desired, brush with egg wash (beat egg with 1 tablespoon water).

10. Bake for 20 to 25 minutes.

Tips or Shaping & Handling Dough

Once you have divided the risen dough into equal portions, roll each portion into a slightly flattened ball. Using a floured finger, punch a hole in the middle and gently pull to enlarge the hole to 2 inches; make the hole larger than you think necessary because it will close up when boiled. Use a bench scraper or large, thin metal spatula to transfer the soft dough to the boiling-water bath.

WHOLE WHEAT BAGELS

These 100 percent whole wheat bagels are rustic yet delicious and take just two cooking steps—boiling and baking. They're chewy and wholesome and make a great breakfast or afternoon snack. Freeze excess bagels, and when you're ready to eat them, defrost in the microwave and pop into the toaster oven for a few minutes. **Yields 12 to 14 pieces**

INGREDIENTS

2¼ teaspoons active dry yeast

2 tablespoons honey

2 cups warm water

4 to 5 cups whole wheat flour, divided

2 teaspoons salt

Poppy seeds, sesame seeds, or dried onions, for sprinkling (optional)

WATER BATH

3½ quarts water

1 teaspoon salt

1. In a large bowl, combine yeast and honey with the warm water and let sit for 5 minutes, until foamy. Add 2 cups of flour and the salt; stir the mixture until a soft dough is formed. Turn dough onto a floured work surface and knead, adding up to 3 more cups of flour as necessary, to form a firm dough that is not sticky. Cover with a towel and let rise until doubled in size, about 1½ hours.

2. Punch down the dough and knead again for a few minutes. Divide the finished dough into 12 to 14 even pieces and roll them into cylinders about 6 inches long. Shape the cylinders into rings and moisten the ends slightly with water to fasten them securely together.

3. Put the water bath on to boil. After the shaped rings have been allowed to rise for about 15 minutes, drop them into the water, 3 at a time, and boil for 3 minutes, turning often. Transfer to a wire rack to drain. Place the boiled bagels on a well-greased baking sheet.

4. Preheat oven to 425°F.

5. If desired, sprinkle poppy seeds, sesame seeds, or dried onions over the bagels and bake for 25 minutes, until golden brown.

PUMPKIN-SPICE BAGELS

For a spicy-sweet brunch treat, make these bagels in the fall. Toast and slather with cream cheese or honey butter. While you're at it, make a double or triple batch and freeze for later. **Yields 8 pieces**

INGREDIENTS

4 cups bread flour, divided

4 teaspoons active dry yeast

1 cup warm water

1½ teaspoons salt

½ cup firmly packed brown sugar

¾ cup puréed pumpkin (see page 84)

2 teaspoons ground cinnamon

1½ teaspoons ground nutmeg

1 teaspoon ground cloves (optional)

1 teaspoon allspice

1 egg (optional)

WATER BATH

1 gallon water

1 tablespoon sugar

1. In a large bowl, combine 2 cups flour and yeast.

2. In a separate bowl, combine warm water, salt, brown sugar, pumpkin, and spices; combine with flour mixture.

3. In a stand mixer with the paddle attachment, beat at low speed for about 30 seconds, scraping the sides of the bowl; beat for an additional 3 minutes on high speed. Incorporate as much of the remaining flour as possible.

4. Turn out dough onto a lightly floured work surface. Knead in additional flour to make a moderately stiff dough. Knead until smooth and elastic. Cover with plastic wrap or a lint-free cotton or linen tea towel (terry cloth will stick and leave lint on the dough) and allow to rest for 15 minutes.

5. Divide dough into 8 equal portions and roll into balls. Punch a hole in the middle with a floured finger and gently pull to enlarge the hole to 2 inches.

6. Place bagels on a greased baking sheet; cover with plastic wrap or a lint-free cotton or linen tea towel and allow to rise for 20 minutes.

7. Meanwhile, heat oven to broil. Prepare the water bath and put it on to boil.

8. After bagels have risen for 20 minutes, broil for 1½ minutes on each side. Reduce oven to 400°F.

9. Once the water bath is boiling, reduce heat. Place bagels, 3 at a time, in water for 1½ minutes, turning after 45 seconds.

10. Drain and place on greased baking sheet. If desired, brush with egg wash (beat egg with 1 tablespoon water).

11. Bake for 25 minutes.

JALAPEÑO BAGELS

Who doesn't love a spicy-hot jalapeño bagel? For variation, add ½ cup cheese (Parmesan or sharp cheddar) to the dough for a jalapeño-cheese bagel. After they've been boiled, top each bagel with additional cheese before baking. Delicious! **Yields 8 pieces**

INGREDIENTS

1½ cups warm water

4 teaspoons active dry yeast

1½ teaspoons salt

1 tablespoon sugar

4 cups bread flour

⅓ cup seeded and minced fresh jalapeños

1 tablespoon plus 1 teaspoon hot red pepper flakes

1 egg, for egg wash (optional)

WATER BATH

1 gallon water

1 tablespoon sugar

1. In a large bowl, combine warm water, yeast, salt, and 1 tablespoon sugar. Add flour, jalapeños, and red pepper flakes; mix into a ball.

2. Turn out onto a lightly floured work surface. Knead for 10 to 12 minutes, adding more flour if necessary, until dough is stiff. Let dough rest for 10 minutes.

3. Divide into 8 equal pieces and form into balls. Punch a hole in the middle with a floured finger and gently pull to enlarge the hole to 2 inches.

4. Place bagels on a greased baking sheet; cover with plastic wrap or a lint-free linen or cotton tea towel (terry cloth will stick and leave lint on the dough) and allow to rise for 20 minutes.

5. Meanwhile, heat oven to broil. Prepare the water bath and put it on to boil.

6. After bagels have risen for 20 minutes, broil for 1½ minutes on each side.

7. Once the water bath is boiling, reduce heat. Place bagels, 3 at a time, in water for 1½ minutes, turning after 45 seconds. Reduce oven temperature to 400°F.

8. Drain and place on greased baking sheet. If desired, brush with egg wash (beat egg with 1 tablespoon water).

9. Bake for 18 to 20 minutes.

SOFT PRETZELS

Making pretzels from scratch is a multistage process. They aren't a snap to make (especially when it comes to rolling and shaping), but they aren't microsurgery either. After bringing together the dough, there's shaping, rising, boiling, and baking. Don't be discouraged by all the steps, but at the same time, give it your full concentration. Don't expect to just whip these out while chatting up company in the kitchen. Give yourself a few quiet hours to assemble your equipment and ingredients, play with your dough, and bake the finished little masterpieces. **Yields 8 pieces**

INGREDIENTS

1½ cups warm water

2½ teaspoons active dry yeast

1 tablespoon sugar

3½ cups all-purpose flour

1 tablespoon salt

Kosher salt, for sprinkling

WATER BATH

1 gallon water

1 tablespoon baking soda

EGG WASH

1 egg

1 tablespoon water

1. In a large bowl, combine warm water, yeast, and sugar; let sit for 5 minutes, until foamy.

2. In a separate bowl, combine flour and salt. Add to yeast mixture and mix until it comes together. Use your hands to combine into a ball. On a lightly floured work surface, knead dough for a few minutes until a smooth, sticky dough forms.

3. Place dough in an oiled bowl and cover with plastic wrap or a lint-free cotton or linen tea towel (terry cloth will stick and leave lint on the dough). Let sit for about 45 minutes.

4. On a lightly floured work surface, divide dough into 8 equal pieces. Roll each piece into a long rope, 18 to 20 inches long. (Don't over-flour your hands or the work surface, as this will make the pieces more difficult to roll.) Twist each piece into a pretzel shape by placing the arc of the pretzel at the bottom (closest to you). Round the two ends so they're facing the arc and twist them around; "paste" them to opposite sides of the arc, using a little water, if necessary. Place on a baking sheet covered with parchment paper.

5. Prepare the water bath. Once boiling, use a slotted spatula to transfer each pretzel into the water and let boil for 3 minutes, flipping once halfway through. Drain on a wire rack and transfer parboiled pretzels back to parchment-lined baking sheet.

6. Preheat oven to 400°F. Make the egg wash by beating the ingredients together. Generously brush over each pretzel and sprinkle with coarse or kosher salt.

7. Bake for 25 minutes, until golden brown.

Tips for Shaping & Handling Dough

Once you have divided the risen dough into equal portions, roll each piece into a long rope, about 18 to 20 inches long. Don't over-flour your hands or the work surface, as it will make the pieces more difficult to roll. Twist each piece into a pretzel shape by placing the arc of the pretzel at the bottom (closest to you). Round the two ends so they're facing the arc, and twist them around each other once. "Paste" them to opposite sides of the arc, using a little water, if necessary. Use a bench scraper or large, thin metal spatula to transfer the soft dough to the boiling-water bath.

Just Top It

For some variety, top your pretzels—after boiling, before baking—with any of the following. Remember that hard seeds may need to be boiled in water for one to two hours, then squeezed well to remove excess moisture, before they are added.

- Poppy seeds
- Sesame seeds
- Caraway seeds
- Dried onion flakes
- Parmesan cheese
- Cinnamon sugar
- Chopped nuts

SOURDOUGH PRETZELS

Once you have eaten a soft sourdough pretzel, all other pretzels will pale in comparison. These chewy bundles of delight are perfect dipped in whole-grain mustard, washed down with a hearty beer. If you are lucky enough to live near a good, German-style bakery, go purchase some pretzels right now and call it research. If not, you can get straight to making them yourself.

Because this dough is fairly dry, it will be easier to prepare using a stand mixer. However, it can still be expertly prepared by hand, and kneading is excellent exercise! **Yields 12 pieces**

INGREDIENTS

2 cups sourdough starter (see page 48)

1 teaspoon salt

1½ tablespoons barley malt syrup

1 cup unbleached, all-purpose flour

1½ cups bread flour

½ cup rye flour

¾ to 1 cup warm water

¼ cup baking soda, for water bath

Kosher or flake salt, for sprinkling

Sesame or poppy seeds, for sprinkling

1. In the bowl of a stand mixer fitted with paddle attachment, combine all ingredients. Mix well to combine, followed by kneading with dough hook for 8 to 10 minutes. Alternatively, knead by hand until smooth and elastic, about 15 minutes. Transfer dough to a greased bowl, cover and let rise in a warm place until almost doubled, 2 to 4 hours.

2. Turn dough onto a lightly floured work surface. Gently fold dough to deflate. Cut the dough into 12 equal pieces. Roll each piece into a long rope, 18 to 20 inches long. Twist each piece into a pretzel shape by placing the arc of the pretzel at the bottom (closest to you). Round the two ends so they're facing the arc and twist them around; "paste" them to opposite sides of the arc, using a little water, if necessary. Set each pretzel on a parchment-lined baking sheet. Cover and let rise in a warm place for 1 to 2 hours, until puffy.

3. Preheat oven to 425°F. Meanwhile, bring a large pot of water to a boil. Carefully add ¼ cup baking soda to the boiling water; it will bubble up.

4. Using a slotted spatula, gently remove pretzels from the baking pan and slide into the boiling water. Simmer about 30 seconds, turn and simmer an additional 30 seconds. Remove with the slotted spatula and return to the baking sheet. Repeat with remaining pretzels.

5. Sprinkle pretzels with kosher or flake salt, or sesame or poppy seeds. Bake for 20 to 30 minutes, until golden brown.

6. Sourdough pretzels, like other sourdough breads, will stay fresh on the counter for up to a week, but they can also be frozen; the salt will dissolve when you thaw them out, leaving polka-dots on your pretzels. They'll still taste great; they just won't be as pretty.

MASHED-POTATO DUMPLINGS

Dumplings are a food made from small pieces of dough, cooked by boiling in liquid, such as water, soup, or stew. Partially submerged in the soup, the dumplings expand as they cook, resulting in a moist little ball that's airy and light on the inside. This recipe is great to use when you have a big bowl of leftover mashed potatoes (like the day after Thanksgiving) and gravy to pour on top. **Yields 10 pieces**

INGREDIENTS

2½ cups mashed or riced
    potatoes

2 teaspoons salt

1 egg

2½ cups all-purpose flour

1. Place the mashed potatoes in a large bowl. Add the salt and egg to the potatoes and mix well.

2. Stir in the flour. Turn dough onto a floured work surface and knead until flour is incorporated; the dough will be stiff. With your hands, roll the dough like a rope into lengths 1 inch thick. Using a sharp knife, cut ropes into 2½-inch-long pieces.

3. Fill a large pot with water one-half to three-quarters full. Over medium-high heat, heat water to boiling; reduce heat to medium-low for continuing boil. Drop dumplings into the pot, stirring gently once with a wooden spoon to keep dumplings from sticking to the bottom.

4. Cook 10 to 12 minutes, until dumplings are cooked through. Remove from pot with a slotted spoon and place on a serving platter. Sprinkle with fresh parsley, or serve with butter or gravy, if desired.

HERBED CORNMEAL DUMPLINGS

These herbed dumplings are excellent with beef stew or chili. For beef stew, use dried oregano; for chili, use fresh cilantro to complement the spicy flavor. **Yields 12 pieces**

INGREDIENTS

1 cup fine cornmeal

1 cup all-purpose flour

4 teaspoons baking powder

½ teaspoon salt

2 tablespoons chopped fresh
    herbs, such as tarragon,
    parsley, thyme, sage, dill,
    or basil

¾ cup milk

1. In a large bowl, sift together cornmeal, flour, baking powder, and salt. Stir in herbs.

2. Add milk and mix to form a soft dough, adding more milk if necessary. Let stand for 5 minutes.

3. Drop by tablespoons into boiling stew and cook for 20 minutes.

MOTHER'S DUMPLINGS

This is a great all-purpose dumpling for special suppers like chicken and dumplings, or an easy way to dress up a plain broth or everyday soup. **Yields 12 pieces**

INGREDIENTS

2 eggs

⅔ cup milk

2 tablespoons unsalted butter, melted

2 cups sifted all-purpose flour

2½ teaspoons baking powder

¾ teaspoon salt

1 tablespoon sugar

Hot broth or soup

1. In a large bowl, beat eggs, milk, and butter. Add flour, baking powder, salt, and sugar; mix lightly. Set aside for 5 minutes to tighten.

2. To a pot of hot broth or soup, drop dough by tablespoonfuls, dipping the spoon into the broth each time before dipping into dough. Cook uncovered for 10 minutes; cover and cook for 10 more minutes, until done. Serve with soup.

OLD-FASHIONED APPLE DUMPLINGS

Dough wrapped around a filling—in this case an apple half—creates a different type of dumpling. For extra flavor, place a small pat of butter and some cinnamon sugar on top of the apple half before sealing the dough around it. **Yields 12 servings**

INGREDIENTS

1½ cups all-purpose flour

2 teaspoons baking powder

1 tablespoon unsalted butter, chilled

½ cup milk

6 apples, peeled

1. In a large bowl, sift the flour and baking powder. Using your fingers, work in the butter until well mixed. Stir in milk. Turn dough onto a floured work surface. Pat and roll to about ¼ inch thick.

2. Cut peeled apples in halves, removing seeds. Cut dough into rounds large enough to enclose apple halves. Fold dough over the apple half and press to seal.

3. Place apple dumplings in a buttered steamer and cook over boiling water for 20 minutes; or bring 3 quarts of water to a boil and lower the dumplings into the water; simmer for 20 minutes, covered, without lifting the lid; remove with a slotted spoon and drain briefly in a colander.

4. Serve dumplings with ice cream and cinnamon sugar.

CIDER VINEGAR DUMPLINGS

These sweet-and-sour dessert dumplings are a real treat, and not at all difficult to prepare. **Yields 12 pieces**

DUMPLINGS

1 cup all-purpose flour

1½ teaspoons baking powder

½ teaspoon salt

2 tablespoons lard or unsalted butter, chilled

½ cup plus 2 tablespoons milk

SAUCE

½ cup cider vinegar

2 cups water

1 cup sugar

¼ teaspoon salt

1 teaspoon vanilla extract

1. In a large bowl, combine flour, baking powder, and salt. Using a pastry blender or two knives, cut in the lard or butter until mixture resembles coarse meal. Add milk and mix; set aside.

2. In a 2-quart saucepan, combine vinegar, water, sugar, salt, and vanilla. Bring to a boil. Drop dough by teaspoonfuls into the boiling liquid and let simmer for 10 minutes. Cover and simmer 10 more minutes.

3. Spoon dumplings into dessert dishes; ladle sauce over dumplings. Serve warm, with whipped cream or ice cream, if desired.

HOT CARAMEL DUMPLINGS

Savory dumplings are for soups and stews, but did you know there are sweet dumplings made for dessert? It's true, and they're perfect served with ice cream. This old-fashioned, uncommon dessert will delight and surprise your guests. **Yields 18 pieces**

SAUCE

2 tablespoons butter

1½ cups firmly packed brown sugar

1½ cups boiling water

Pinch salt

DUMPLINGS

1¼ cups all-purpose flour

1½ teaspoons baking powder

⅓ cup granulated sugar

2 tablespoons unsalted butter, chilled

½ cup milk

½ teaspoon vanilla extract

1. In a medium saucepan over medium heat, combine butter with brown sugar, boiling water, and salt. Cook, stirring constantly, until sugar dissolves and butter melts. Reduce heat to low, stirring occasionally, as dumplings are being prepared.

2. In a medium bowl, sift flour with baking powder and sugar. With a pastry blender or two knives, cut in butter until mixture resembles coarse meal. Add milk and vanilla; mix until just moistened.

3. Drop dough by teaspoonfuls into hot caramel sauce. Cover tightly and cook over medium-low heat for 20 minutes. Do not remove cover during cooking.

4. Spoon dumplings into dessert dishes; ladle sauce over dumplings. Serve warm, with whipped cream or ice cream, if desired.

Doughnuts & Other Fried Breads

. . . .

Frying bread is a more advanced method of bread making, but one you can easily master with a little bit of practice. Take notes on what works for you in your kitchen—the elements of temperature and humidity come into play here. Also, when frying these delicacies, consider our favorite fat: home-rendered lard made from the fat of pastured hogs. Contrary to popular belief, it's now considered healthy again since it's made up of about 40 percent saturated fat, 48 percent monounsaturated fat, and 12 percent polyunsaturated fat. Plus, home-rendered lard is not hydrogenated, like store-bought brands are. The amount of omega-6 and omega-3 fatty acids varies in lard according to what the pigs have eaten, making fat from pastured or grass-fed hogs the best choice. Lard is also a good source of vitamin D. Lard is absolutely the best fat for frying; with a smoke point between 370°F and 390°F, very little oxidation takes place during the process, and nothing crisps food like lard. So fire up that kettle with some good old-fashioned lard!

POTATO DROP DOUGHNUTS

Where did doughnuts come from? Washington Irving's reference to "doughnuts" in 1809 in his *History of New York* is usually cited as the first recorded use of the term. He described "balls of sweetened dough, fried in hog's fat, and called doughnuts, or *olykoeks*" (a Dutch word meaning "oil cakes"). These "nuts" of fried dough are what we now call doughnut holes. Enjoy these little nuggets of sweetness. **Yields 3 dozen doughnuts**

INGREDIENTS

Lard or oil, for deep frying

4 cups all-purpose flour

4 teaspoons baking powder

½ teaspoon salt

1 teaspoon ground nutmeg or cinnamon

2 tablespoons virgin coconut oil, melted

1 cup mashed potatoes

2 eggs, beaten

1⅓ cups granulated sugar

1 cup milk

1 teaspoon vanilla extract

Granulated or powdered sugar, for rolling

1. Heat 1 inch of lard or oil in a large kettle to 370°F.

2. In a large bowl, sift flour, baking powder, salt, and nutmeg or cinnamon together. In a separate bowl, combine oil, potatoes, eggs, sugar, milk, and vanilla. Add dry ingredients to the liquids, 1 cup at a time, mixing well.

3. Drop dough by teaspoon into hot lard or oil, and fry until golden brown, about 3 minutes, on all sides. Remove from oil and roll as desired in additional sugar, cinnamon sugar, or powdered sugar.

Tips or Shaping & Handling Dough

When rolling out the dough, use all the tools that might help: a floured or covered rolling pin, a floured silicone pastry mat, and even a tool called a doughnut cutter—a round biscuit cutter with a circle in the middle. In lieu of a doughnut cutter, use a biscuit cutter and make the inner circle by hand with a knife or rim of a small bottle (a beer bottle works well). Again, use a bench scraper or thin metal spatula to transfer the soft dough into the hot oil.

APPLESAUCE DROP DOUGHNUTS

These delicious little "nuts" are dredged in melted butter and cinnamon sugar. Your family and friends will love them, so make plenty for seconds and thirds. **Yields 2½ dozen doughnuts**

INGREDIENTS

Lard or oil, for deep frying

2 cups all-purpose flour

1½ cups sugar, divided

2 teaspoons baking powder

½ teaspoon salt

2 teaspoons ground cinnamon, divided

1 egg

½ cup applesauce

½ cup milk

1½ tablespoons virgin coconut oil, melted,

½ cup unsalted butter

1. Heat 1 inch of lard or oil in a large kettle to 365°F.

2. In a large bowl, sift flour, ½ cup sugar, baking powder, salt, and 1 teaspoon cinnamon together. In a small bowl, beat egg; add applesauce, milk, and oil. Stir applesauce mixture into sifted ingredients and mix well.

3. Drop dough by teaspoonfuls into hot lard or oil; fry to golden brown, about 3 minutes, on all sides. Transfer to a paper-towel-lined plate.

4. Place the butter in a medium bowl and melt in the microwave. Combine remaining sugar and cinnamon in another bowl and mix well.

5. While the doughnuts are still warm, dunk quickly in the melted butter, then dredge in the cinnamon sugar. Serve immediately.

PUFF BALLS

These plain doughnut holes are easy to make and will always please a crowd. Don't get overzealous and make the puffs too large, though, or they will not cook through. **Yields 2½ dozen doughnuts**

INGREDIENTS

Lard or oil, for deep frying

2 cups all-purpose flour

¼ cup granulated sugar

3 teaspoons baking powder

1 teaspoon salt

1 teaspoon ground nutmeg or mace

¼ cup virgin coconut oil, melted

¾ cup milk

1 egg

Powdered sugar, for dusting

1. Heat 1 inch of lard or oil in a large kettle to 365°F.

2. In a large bowl, sift together the flour, sugar, baking powder, salt, and nutmeg. Add the oil, milk, and egg; stir with fork until thoroughly mixed.

3. Drop by teaspoonfuls into the hot lard or oil; fry until golden brown on all sides, about 3 minutes. Transfer to a paper-towel-lined plate. Dust with powdered sugar and serve immediately.

ANGEL DOUGHNUTS

After the doughnut hole came the larger ringed doughnut—but how? A sixteen-year-old American boy named Hanson Gregory is believed to have invented the ring-shaped doughnut in 1847 aboard a trading ship. The story goes that he was dissatisfied with the greasiness—and often raw centers—of regular doughnuts, so he punched a hole in the center of the dough with the ship's tin pepper box. He later taught the technique to his mother, and now we have what the world calls "doughnuts." This recipe is your basic fried cake doughnut in all its glory. **Yields 1 dozen doughnuts**

INGREDIENTS

Lard or oil, for deep frying

2 eggs

1 teaspoon salt

3 tablespoons lard or unsalted butter, melted and slightly cooled

1 cup milk

4 tablespoons corn syrup

½ cup granulated sugar

6 cups all-purpose flour

4 teaspoons baking powder

½ teaspoon ground nutmeg

Powdered sugar, for sprinkling

1. Heat 2 inches of lard or oil in a large kettle to 365°F.

2. In a large bowl, mix eggs, salt, lard or butter, milk, corn syrup, and sugar together thoroughly. Sift flour, baking powder, and nutmeg together; add to wet mixture, stirring thoroughly. Do not beat.

3. Roll dough out on a floured work surface to ½ inch thick, and cut with a biscuit or doughnut cutter.

4. Fry in hot lard or oil until golden brown on both sides, about 3 minutes. Drain on a paper-towel-lined plate. Sprinkle with powdered sugar.

PUMPKIN DOUGHNUTS

These are delicious, fried cake doughnuts, reminiscent of fall and pumpkin pie. Top with granulated or powdered sugar as called for, or make a simple glaze of 3 tablespoons melted butter, 1 cup powdered sugar, and 2 tablespoons pure maple syrup; drizzle or dip the doughnut tops in it. What a treat! **Yields ½ dozen doughnuts**

INGREDIENTS

3 cups all-purpose flour

1¼ teaspoons pumpkin pie spice

1¼ teaspoons salt

¾ teaspoon baking soda

½ teaspoon cream of tartar

2 tablespoons lard or butter

¾ cup firmly packed brown sugar

4 egg yolks, or 2 whole eggs plus 1 egg yolk, beaten

1 cup puréed pumpkin (see page 84)

¼ cup sour cream

Lard or oil, for deep frying

Granulated or powdered sugar, for dusting

1. In a large bowl, sift together the flour, pumpkin pie spice, salt, baking soda, and cream of tartar; set aside.

2. In a separate large bowl, cream together the lard or butter and brown sugar until well blended, about 3 minutes. Add eggs and mix well. Add pumpkin and sour cream and mix thoroughly. Add dry ingredients to pumpkin mixture and mix until smooth.

3. With minimal handling, roll dough on floured board until ⅓ inch thick. Let stand 20 minutes.

4. Heat 2 inches of lard or oil in a large kettle to 365°F.

5. Cut dough with 2½-inch biscuit or doughnut cutter and fry in hot oil or lard until light brown, turning when the first crack appears. Drain on a paper-towel-lined plate.

6. When doughnuts are cool, shake in paper bag with granulated or powdered sugar to coat.

BANANA DOUGHNUTS

Banana doughnuts are yummy, but how about banana doughnuts topped with peanut butter glaze? Whisk together 2 tablespoons creamy peanut butter with 2 tablespoons warm water and 1 cup powdered sugar. Spread it on the warm doughnuts. **Yields 2 dozen doughnuts**

INGREDIENTS

Lard or oil, for deep frying

5 cups sifted all-purpose flour

3 tablespoons baking powder

1 teaspoon baking soda

2 teaspoons salt

1 teaspoon ground nutmeg

¼ cup lard or unsalted butter, softened

1 cup granulated sugar

3 eggs

1½ teaspoons vanilla extract

¾ cup mashed bananas

½ cup buttermilk or sour milk (see page 40)

Powdered sugar, for dusting

1. Heat 2 inches of lard or oil in a large kettle to 365°F.

2. In a large bowl, re-sift flour with baking powder, baking soda, salt, and nutmeg.

3. In a separate large bowl, cream the lard or butter with the sugar for 3 minutes; add eggs and beat smooth. Add vanilla, bananas, and buttermilk; beat well. Add flour mixture and stir until smooth.

4. Turn small portions of dough onto a floured work surface. Knead lightly; roll to ⅜ inch thick and cut with a biscuit or doughnut cutter. Fry in hot lard or oil until golden brown, about 3 minutes, turning once. Transfer to a paper-towel-lined plate. Dust with powdered sugar.

GLAZED AND RAISED POTATO DOUGHNUTS

Doughnuts first came onto the American food scene in the early nineteenth century, and according to anthropologist Paul R. Mullins, the first cookbook mentioning doughnuts was an 1803 English volume that included doughnuts in an appendix of American recipes. By the mid-nineteenth century, this food looked and tasted like today's doughnut and was viewed as a thoroughly American food. Now this is something to be proud of! **Yields 3 dozen doughnuts**

INGREDIENTS

2¼ teaspoons active dry yeast

¼ cup plus 6 tablespoons warm water, divided

1 cup milk, scalded

¼ cup lard or unsalted butter, softened

¼ cup granulated sugar

1 teaspoon salt

¾ cup mashed potatoes

2 eggs, beaten

5 to 6 cups sifted all-purpose flour

Lard or oil, for deep frying

1 pound powdered sugar

1 tablespoon vanilla extract

1. Dissolve yeast in ¼ cup warm water. In a large bowl, combine milk, lard or butter, sugar, and salt; cool to lukewarm. Stir in potatoes and eggs. Gradually add enough flour to make a soft dough.

2. Turn dough onto a floured work surface and knead until smooth and satiny. Place in a lightly greased bowl; turn dough to grease top. Cover and let rise in a warm place until doubled in size, 1 to 1½ hours.

3. Roll dough out to ½ inch thick and cut with a 3-inch doughnut cutter. Cover and let rise until doubled in size, about 30 minutes.

4. Heat 2 inches of lard or oil in a large kettle to 370°F.

5. Meanwhile, stir powdered sugar, remaining 6 tablespoons water, and vanilla together to make a glaze. Mixture will look like very thick cream.

6. Fry doughnuts in batches until golden brown. Drain on a paper-towel-lined plate. Dip tops of doughnuts into glaze; place on a wire rack until glaze is set.

ITALIAN FRIED DOUGHNUTS

These doughnuts are Grandma Grimaldi approved and easy to make. Italians traditionally serve them on the Feast of St. Joseph (March 19), at Easter, and on picnics. They are usually served for dessert with coffee, but rarely for breakfast. They're delicious with fresh jam and served piping hot. **Yields 2 dozen doughnuts**

INGREDIENTS

6 cups white whole wheat flour

2 teaspoons active dry yeast

2 teaspoons salt

¼ cup granulated sugar

3 eggs

¼ cup olive oil

2½ cups lukewarm water

1 quart lard or oil, for deep frying

Powdered or cinnamon sugar for dusting

1. In the bowl of a stand mixer, add flour, yeast, salt, and sugar. In a small bowl, beat the eggs with the olive oil. Attach the dough hook, turn on the mixer to low, and mix the dry ingredients. With the mixer running, add the egg/oil mixture and as much water as needed to bring the dough together. The dough should be sticky but hold together.

2. Knead the dough by machine for about 10 minutes; scrape down the mixing bowl a few times during the kneading.

3. Cover the dough with a damp cloth and allow it to rise in a warm location for about 2 hours. When the dough has risen, oil your hands with a little olive oil and sprinkle the counter with a bit of flour. Punch down the dough. To form the doughnuts, pinch small pieces of dough and form into balls about half as big as you want your finished doughnuts to be. Palm size is just about right, but some people like them smaller.

4. Allow the doughnuts to rise, covered with a lint-free cotton or linen tea towel (terry cloth will stick and leave lint on the dough), for about half an hour.

5. Meanwhile, heat 2 inches of lard or oil in a large kettle to 370°F.

6. Fry doughnuts in batches in hot oil, being careful not to overcrowd them; fry for about 3 minutes per side until they are golden brown. Drain on a paper-towel-lined plate.

7. Sprinkle doughnuts with powdered sugar or roll them in cinnamon sugar.

MALASADAS (PORTUGUESE DOUGHNUTS)

The *malasada* originated on the island of São Miguel. When the first Portuguese immigrants moved from the island in the late 1800s to Hawaii to work on the sugarcane plantations, they brought malasadas with them. Today, malasadas have been adopted into Hawaiian cuisine and are extremely popular in many parts of the islands. These bite-sized fritters of fried dough are puffy and crispy—and just heavenly. **Yields 7 dozen doughnuts**

INGREDIENTS

2¼ teaspoons active dry yeast

½ cup plus 1 teaspoon sugar, divided

¼ cup warm water

6 cups all-purpose flour

6 eggs, beaten

¼ cup butter or lard, melted

1 cup evaporated milk

1 teaspoon salt

Lard or oil, for deep frying

1. Dissolve yeast and 1 teaspoon sugar in ¼ cup warm water. Measure the flour into a large bowl and make a well in the center. Add yeast mixture, eggs, butter or lard, evaporated milk, and salt. Beat thoroughly to form a soft dough. Cover bowl with a towel and let rise until doubled, about 1 to 1½ hours.

2. Heat 2 inches of lard or oil in a large kettle to 370°F.

3. With a teaspoon, spoon dough carefully from bowl to keep dough from dripping. Drop into hot oil or lard and fry until brown, 3 to 4 minutes, on all sides. Drain on a paper-towel-lined plate.

4. Place remaining ½ cup sugar in a bag; shake doughnuts in sugar. Serve hot or cold.

MOLASSES DOUGHNUTS

Sweetened only with natural molasses, these doughnuts will not taste as sweet as what you're used to, but old-timers will love the flavors reminiscent of days gone by. **Yields 3 dozen**

INGREDIENTS

Lard or oil, for deep frying

7 cups all-purpose flour

2 teaspoons salt

1 teaspoon baking soda

4 teaspoons baking powder

½ teaspoon ground ginger

1 teaspoon ground nutmeg

2 teaspoons ground cinnamon

1 egg

1½ cups unsulfured molasses

½ cup milk

2 tablespoons unsalted butter, melted

Powdered sugar, for dusting

1. Heat 2 inches of lard or oil in a large kettle to 370°F.

2. In a large bowl, sift flour with salt, baking soda, baking powder, and spices. In a separate bowl, beat the egg and molasses; add the milk and butter. Add the dry ingredients and mix thoroughly.

3. Turn dough onto a floured work surface. Roll out to ½ inch thick and cut with a 3-inch doughnut cutter.

4. Fry in batches in hot lard or oil until brown, 3 to 4 minutes, on all sides; drain on a paper-towel-lined plate. Dust with powdered sugar.

CORN FRITTERS

In the United States, fritters are small cakes made from flour or cornmeal batter consisting of a primary ingredient (like apples or corn) mixed with eggs and milk, and then deep fried. Corn fritters are popular all over the world, but particularly in the southern United States. They are especially delicious when made in the summer with fresh sweet corn. Serve hot, with maple syrup drizzled over the top, or on the side for dipping. **Yields 24 pieces**

INGREDIENTS

Lard or oil, for deep frying

1⅓ cups sifted all-purpose flour

1½ teaspoons baking powder

¾ teaspoon salt

Black pepper, to taste

⅔ cup milk

1 egg, well beaten

1½ cups whole-kernel corn, drained

1. Heat 1 inch of lard or oil in a kettle to 365°F.

2. In a large bowl, sift together the flour, baking powder, and salt. Season with black pepper. In a separate bowl, blend milk and egg; add gradually to the dry ingredients. Stir in the corn.

3. Drop dough by the tablespoon into the hot oil or lard and fry for 2 to 5 minutes, turning once. Remove with a slotted spoon and drain on a paper-towel-lined plate.

APPLESAUCE FRITTERS

Dust these moist fritters with powdered sugar or make a simple glaze to drizzle on while they're still warm.
Yields 48 pieces

INGREDIENTS

Lard or oil for deep frying

2¼ cups all-purpose flour

1½ teaspoons baking powder

½ teaspoon baking soda

½ teaspoon ground cinnamon

½ teaspoon ground nutmeg

½ teaspoon ground cloves

¼ teaspoon salt

½ cup granulated sugar

¼ cup firmly packed brown sugar

2 eggs

2 tablespoons virgin coconut oil, melted

¼ cup milk

1 cup unsweetened applesauce

½ teaspoon vanilla extract

1. Heat 2 inches of lard or oil in a large kettle to 360°F.

2. In a large bowl, sift together the flour, baking powder, baking soda, cinnamon, nutmeg, cloves, and salt. In a separate bowl, beat together the sugar, brown sugar, and eggs with an electric mixer at medium speed until mixture is fluffy. Beat in coconut oil. Stir in flour mixture alternately with milk, beginning and ending with dry ingredients. Mix well. Stir in applesauce and vanilla.

3. Carefully drop batter by level tablespoonfuls, three or four at a time, into hot oil. Fry, turning once, for 3 minutes, or until golden. Remove with a slotted spoon and drain on a paper-towel-lined plate.

FRIED CORNBREAD

This is a delightful twist on plain old cornbread, like a cross between cornbread and a hushpuppy. As you fry your way through the batter, keep the cakes warm in the oven until you are ready to serve. Serve with whipped honey butter. **Yields 6 pieces**

INGREDIENTS

1 cup white cornmeal

½ cup self-rising flour

1 teaspoon salt

½ to ¾ cup boiling water

Lard or oil for frying

1. In a large bowl, sift together the cornmeal, flour, and salt. Stir in enough boiling water to make a stiff dough. While dough is still hot, scoop out a golf ball–size piece. Wet your palm and roll and flatten the dough; the cake should be biscuit shaped. Repeat procedure for remaining dough.

2. Heat ¼ inch of lard or oil in a skillet over medium heat until hot. Fry cornbread to a golden brown on both sides, adding oil between batches as needed. Drain on paper towels.

INDIAN FRY BREAD

Contrary to popular belief, fry bread is not an indigenous Native American food, as it did not exist during pre-Columbian times. According to the Navajo, fry bread became a diet staple when they used the flour, sugar, salt, and lard that was given to them by the United States government, and to this day it is often served both at home and at gatherings, with many different recipes existing among the tribes. Most fry bread recipes do not contain yeast, because it was not typically available to native peoples when this foodstuff was developed.

Fry bread can be eaten alone or with various toppings such as honey or jam. It can also be made into "Indian tacos," where it's used as a base for beef, beans, salsa, and cheese. **Yields 18 pieces**

INGREDIENTS

4 cups all-purpose flour

1 teaspoon baking powder

¾ cup nonfat dry milk powder

1 teaspoon salt

2 to 2½ cups warm water

Lard or oil, for deep frying

1. In a large bowl, combine flour, baking powder, milk powder, and salt. Add enough warm water to form a soft dough, mixing well. Cover and set aside to rise for 2 to 3 hours.

2. Heat 1 inch of lard or oil in a large kettle to 365°F.

3. Turn dough onto a floured work surface and knead for 1 minute. Pinch off ¼-cup-size pieces and roll out.

4. Fry pieces of dough in hot oil or lard until lightly browned. Drain on a paper-towel-lined plate. Serve warm.

HUSHPUPPIES

How did this fried ball of cornmeal get the name "hushpuppy"? According to popular culture, it's often attributed to hunters and fishermen who fried a basic cornmeal mixture and fed it to their dogs to "hush the puppies" during cookouts or fish fries. Other stories date the term to the Civil War, in which soldiers are claimed to have tossed fried cornbread to quell the barks of Confederate dogs. Whatever the origin, we love hushpuppies, especially dipped in a creamy mayonnaise sauce. **Yields 3 dozen**

INGREDIENTS

2 cups cornmeal

2 tablespoons all-purpose flour

3½ cups boiling water

2 tablespoons lard, melted

2 tablespoons grated onion

1 teaspoon baking powder

1½ teaspoons salt

½ teaspoon black pepper

1. In a large glass bowl, combine cornmeal and flour. Pour in the boiling water and mix well; set aside to cool.

2. Add lard, onion, baking powder, salt, and pepper. Mix well.

3. Drop by the tablespoonful onto a hot, well-greased griddle, and flatten slightly with a spatula. Cook until well done, about 3 minutes, turning once to cook both sides. Serve immediately.

SOUTHERN-STYLE HUSHPUPPIES

Hushpuppies are native to the southern United States, where they are almost always on the menus of fish restaurants, among other places. Hushpuppies are typically made with cornmeal, wheat flour, eggs, salt, baking soda, milk, or buttermilk and may include onion, garlic, corn, and peppers—or, in this case, okra. The small breads are fried until crispy golden brown. Serve these alongside barbecue in the summer when the okra is ripe in the garden. **Yields 4 dozen**

INGREDIENTS

2 cups cornmeal

1 cup all-purpose flour

2 eggs

1½ cups buttermilk or sour milk (see page 40)

3 medium onions, diced

1 pound okra

Lard or oil, for deep frying

1. In a medium bowl, combine cornmeal and flour. In a second bowl, beat eggs with buttermilk. Stir in onions and mix well; add milk mixture to cornmeal mixture and stir until just combined; a lumpy mixture is fine.

2. Remove stems from okra. Wash and cut into round medallions, approximately ½ inch thick. Stir okra into cornmeal mixture. If mixture seems too dry, add a small amount of cold water until proper consistency. Cover and store in the refrigerator until ready to fry.

3. Heat 1 inch of lard or oil in a large kettle to 370°F.

4. Drop hushpuppies by the tablespoonful into hot oil or lard, using a long-handled spoon. Place the spoon in a glass of warm water when not using. Brown hushpuppies on one side; turn to brown other side. Serve immediately.

Gluten-Free Breads

In the last decade or so, gluten sensitivities and intolerances have become common, and people are increasingly opting to choose gluten-free (GF) options when dining out, doing their grocery shopping, and, of course, cooking at home. According to the Celiac Disease Foundation, one in every one hundred people is affected by celiac disease, an autoimmune disorder in which the small intestine is hypersensitive to gluten. The problem is, 97 percent of the people with it are still undiagnosed, and those who are aware of it may not know where to start when it comes to cooking gluten-free.

What is gluten, you ask? Gluten is a protein found in many products, including wheat, rye, and barley (see "What Is Gluten-Free?" on page 196). If people who have celiac disease consume gluten, their body mounts an immune-system response that attacks the small intestine. After so much damage occurs, nutrients cannot be absorbed properly by the body. It's important to make sure that those with celiac disease do not come in contact with gluten and that there is no cross-contamination of products when preparing foods.

Baking gluten-free will be a bit more challenging than the typical baking you've done in the past. Without the magic of gluten, a new set of ingredients is necessary, batters and doughs will be looser, and the texture of the finished bread will be quite different. But gluten-free baking can be delicious. In this chapter, we'll provide you with a gluten-free sampling of all the various breads in our book: quick breads and muffins; yeasted loaves; rolled breads such as biscuits and cinnamon rolls; flatbreads; and boiled and fried breads such as bagels, pretzels, and doughnuts. Gluten-free doesn't have to be taste-free!

What Is Gluten-Free?

These days, the phrase "gluten-free" seems to be everywhere. Grocery stores (even in our not-so-metropolitan Kansas town) now have gluten-free aisles. But what is gluten, and why does everyone suddenly want to be free of it?

- Gluten is actually an important protein complex in bread and other foods. The Chinese call it "the muscle of flour." Found in wheat and its close relatives, gluten is made up of glutenin and gliadin (in wheat), secalin (in rye), and hordein (in barley). It doesn't dissolve in water and comes from the endosperm—the starchy part of the seed that provides nutrition for the developing plant.

- Gluten plays a celebrated role in bread making. A "gluten network" gives bread its structure and makes the dough elastic enough to rise. Many of the steps in bread making are about creating this network.

- Celebrity chef and author Alton Brown once compared the structure of proteins to old-fashioned coiled phone cords. At the beginning of bread making, a gluten molecule is much like a phone cord that's been well used. It's twisted back on itself, and you may have trouble getting it to stretch at all. Weak bonds have even formed between different areas of the coils to keep it in a folded mass. One way to untangle these phone cords is to add water; this starts the process and allows the cords to unfold.

- Imagine that the ends of these no-longer-tangled phone cords can attach to one another to form long chains. The stretching and folding of kneading allows these now-linear phone cords to align and join together. Once they are side by side, parts of the coils can then connect with each other. You have now created a kind of mesh structure made with chains of coiled gluten proteins in the dough. During the rising phase, yeast adds carbon dioxide bubbles to the dough, which also assists in the lining up and stretching out of the gluten strands. When you put your bubble-filled gluten mesh into the oven, the heat solidifies the gluten and starch, and the structure of bread is formed.

- Gluten is also what makes gravy thick and pasta able to soak up sauce. It's used in some meat substitutes (like seitan), primarily because of its texture and absorbent qualities. These qualities also make it a good candidate for being added to foods that need structure or absorbency—like popsicles and ice cream.

Tips for Gluten-Free Baking

Navigating the new world of gluten-free cooking and baking can be confusing. Here are some tips to help you on your journey.

1. Safe flours: Gluten-free flours include white and brown rice flours (including sweet rice flour), sorghum flour, millet flour, buckwheat flour, quinoa flour, teff flour, and certified gluten-free oat flour. Commercial oats are often milled with wheat crops and, as a result, are cross-contaminated. Purchase oats—and also corn, millet, sorghum—that are labeled "certified gluten-free."

2. Starches: Starches provide tenderness and browning to GF baked goods. Safe starches include potato starch, cornstarch, arrowroot starch, and tapioca starch.

3. Grain-free flours/meals: Nongrain, high-protein flours or meals include almond flour, hazelnut flour, and chestnut flour. Meals are usually a bit more coarse than those labeled "flour," and their use will result in a grainier finished product. Legume flours include chickpea flour and soy flour. Coconut flour adds a lot of texture and flavor, as well as attracting moisture, but should be used in very small quantities.

4. Xanthan gum: It sounds like a scary, made-up thing, but it is vital in GF baking. Xanthan gum adds viscosity and stretch to batters and doughs. What is it exactly? It's a mold-derived additive grown on cellulose (usually corn); it's odorless and tasteless (if it isn't, throw it away). A bag will last for months since it is used in very small quantities; store it in the refrigerator.

5. Baked goods that call for puréed fruit or vegetables (banana or pumpkin breads or muffins), shredded vegetables, and yogurt or sour cream translate well to gluten-free, because these ingredients help wheat-free, gluten-free quick breads and muffins stay moist.

6. Substituting light-brown sugar for refined granulated (white) sugar in recipes will improve flavor and increase moistness.

7. Use extra vanilla extract (even a whole tablespoon). Many gluten-free flours have strong or bland tastes; adding extra vanilla will soften or improve the flavor of your finished product.

8. Bring your ingredients, like eggs, butter, and milk, to room temperature. To quickly warm eggs, set them in warm (not hot) water for a few minutes.

9. Remove loaves and muffins from their pans as quickly as possible—when cool enough to handle safely. Gluten-free baked goods will get soggy the longer they remain in a hot pan.

10. The best resource, hands down, for gluten-free baking and cooking is Karina Allrich, the "Gluten-Free Goddess," at www.glutenfreegoddess.blogspot.com.

GLUTEN-FREE FLOUR MIX I

The majority of gluten-free flour mixes that you can purchase are made from rice flour. When white rice flour is used exclusively, the baked goods tend to turn out on the gummy side. Make this light flour mixture that combines white and brown rice flours for better results. **Yields 5 cups**

INGREDIENTS

1¼ cups white rice flour

1¼ cups brown rice flour

1 cup potato starch

1 cup tapioca flour/starch

¼ cup garbanzo bean flour

¼ cup cornstarch

2½ tablespoons xanthan gum

Sift all the ingredients into a large bowl. Stir ingredients together with a whisk. Store in an airtight container in refrigerator or freezer.

GLUTEN-FREE FLOUR MIX II

This is a medium-weight mix that combines rice flour with sorghum flour. Sorghum flour is a GF favorite because it bakes up so lovely and is soft and slightly sweet. Starches lighten the mix, and potato starch is preferred over tapioca starch because it gives a soft, light rise. Double, triple, or quadruple this recipe to make a larger quantity for later use. **Yields 3 cups**

INGREDIENTS

1 cup rice (white or brown) flour

1 cup sorghum flour

⅔ cup potato starch

⅓ cup tapioca starch

1 teaspoon xanthan gum

Combine all ingredients and mix well. Store in an airtight container in refrigerator or freezer.

GLUTEN-FREE FLOUR MIX III

This is equivalent to an all-purpose flour, perfect for muffins, quick breads, bagels, pretzels, and doughnuts. Multiply this recipe for a larger quantity to freeze. **Yields 2½ cups**

INGREDIENTS

1 cup sorghum flour or gluten-free oat flour

1 cup potato starch (not potato flour)

½ cup almond meal

1 teaspoon xanthan gum

Combine all ingredients and mix well. Store in an airtight container in refrigerator or freezer.

GLUTEN-FREE SANDWICH BREAD

We love this bread made with our Gluten-Free Flour Mix III on page 199 the soft and slightly sweet sorghum flour that dominates the mix turns out a beautiful sandwich loaf. **Yields 1 loaf**

INGREDIENTS

1½ cups milk

4 tablespoons honey

2½ teaspoons active dry yeast

3 cups Gluten-Free Flour Mix III (see page 199)

1½ teaspoons xanthan gum

4 teaspoons baking powder

1 teaspoon salt

2 teaspoons lemon juice

¼ cup olive oil

2 eggs

1. In a 2-cup glass measuring cup, heat the milk in the microwave until it's warm but not hot. Stir in the honey and yeast. Set aside and let proof for about 10 minutes.

2. Meanwhile, in a large bowl, combine the flour mix with xanthan gum, baking powder, and salt; mix well.

3. In the bowl of a stand mixer fitted with a paddle attachment, combine lemon juice, oil, and eggs. Add yeast mixture and mix for a couple of seconds. On medium-high speed, beat in the dry ingredients, beating for 3 to 4 minutes, until dough is wet, thick, and sticky.

4. Transfer dough to a greased and floured 9 x 5-inch loaf pan. Set on the stovetop and let rise until doubled in size, about 20 to 30 minutes, when dough reaches top of pan. Meanwhile, preheat oven to 375°F.

5. Bake for 30 to 45 minutes, until the internal temperature reaches 200–210°F when measured with an instant-read thermometer. If the bread is browning too quickly, cover loosely with foil. Cool in the pan for 5 minutes, then turn bread out onto a wire rack to cool completely before slicing.

6. Store in a plastic bag at room temperature or in the refrigerator.

GLUTEN-FREE FLAX BREAD

This combination of gluten-free flours and wet ingredients turns out a nicely moist and flavorful loaf packed with nutrition. Flaxseeds, eggs, and coconut oil deliver a healthy dose of omega-3s and good fats. **Yields 1 loaf**

INGREDIENTS

1¼ cups Gluten-Free Flour Mix III (see page 199)

¼ cup chickpea flour

½ cup potato starch

¼ cup cornstarch

¼ cup ground flaxseeds

2½ teaspoons xanthan gum

2 teaspoons active dry yeast

1 teaspoon salt

2 eggs

2 egg whites

1 cup water or milk

2 tablespoons virgin coconut oil, melted

2 tablespoons honey

2 teaspoons vinegar

1. Grease a 9 x 5-inch loaf pan with coconut oil; set aside.

2. In a bowl, combine flours, potato starch, cornstarch, flaxseeds, xanthan gum, yeast, and salt.

3. In a large mixing bowl, combine eggs, egg whites, water or milk, oil, honey, and vinegar, and mix well. Add dry ingredients and mix with an electric mixer on medium speed for 4 to 5 minutes, scraping sides of bowl occasionally.

4. Pour mixture into the prepared pan and let rise in warm spot for 1 to 1½ hours, until the dough rises to the top of the pan.

5. Preheat oven to 350°F.

6. Bake for about 40 minutes. Remove from pan and cool completely on a wire rack.

GLUTEN-FREE DINNER ROLLS

These delightful little breads are a cross between a muffin and a roll. Simply combine the ingredients and spoon into muffin cups—no rolling or cutting required. **Yields 12 pieces**

INGREDIENTS

2 cups milk

¼ cup sugar, divided

2 tablespoons active dry yeast

3 cups Gluten-Free Flour Mix II
(see page 199)

2 teaspoons xanthan gum

4 teaspoons baking powder

1 teaspoon salt

2 teaspoons vinegar

2 eggs

¼ cup olive oil

Butter, melted, for brushing

1. Grease a standard muffin pan with melted butter or line with paper cups; set aside.

2. In a small bowl, heat milk to warm but not boiling. Stir in 1 tablespoon sugar. Add yeast and whisk to combine and dissolve. Set aside until mixture is foamy.

3. In a large bowl, combine flour mix, xanthan gum, baking powder, remaining sugar, and salt; set aside.

4. In the bowl of a stand mixer fitted with paddle attachment, beat together the vinegar, eggs, and oil. Add the yeast mixture, then add flour mixture, beating on low until all ingredients are mixed. Increase speed to high and beat for an additional 3 to 5 minutes.

5. Spoon dough into the prepared muffin pan, filling each cup three-quarters full. Dip a sharp knife into a little additional gluten-free flour mix, then cut a slash in each roll. Allow rolls to rise covered with a damp tea towel until doubled in size, about 35 to 40 minutes.

6. Meanwhile, preheat oven to 375°F. Brush the tops of rolls with melted butter, and bake for 20 to 25 minutes, until tops are golden brown. If tops begin browning too quickly, cover loosely with foil. Remove from oven and brush with melted butter again. Let cool in the pan for a few minutes before removing and serving.

GLUTEN-FREE BISCUITS

When you just have to have your standby favorite old-fashioned biscuits, these will do. They won't rise as high as traditional biscuits, but they will be moist and flavorful thanks to the addition of yogurt. **Yields 6 pieces**

INGREDIENTS

1¾ cups Gluten-Free Flour Mix I (see page 198)

1 teaspoon xanthan gum

3 teaspoons baking powder

1 teaspoon baking soda

2 teaspoons sugar

1 teaspoon salt

6 tablespoons unsalted butter, chilled and cut into small pieces

1 cup plain yogurt

1. Preheat oven to 425°F.

2. In a large bowl, combine flour mix, xanthan gum, baking powder, baking soda, sugar, and salt; whisk to blend. Using a pastry blender or two knives, cut in the butter until mixture resembles coarse meal. Add yogurt and mix until the dough forms a ball.

3. Turn dough onto a piece of plastic wrap and pat ¾ inch thick. Cut dough with a 2-inch round biscuit cutter or the rim of a drinking glass, and place biscuits 1 inch apart on an ungreased baking sheet.

4. Bake for 15 to 20 minutes, until golden brown. Serve immediately.

GLUTEN-FREE ROSEMARY-POTATO ROLLS

These dinner rolls are perfect for a GF Thanksgiving or Christmas dinner. The texture and flavor are spot on—no need to make a wheat version as well. If you prefer, instead of cutting the dough into squares, roll it into balls for a true roll shape. Bake the same as the recipe indicates. **Yields 18 pieces**

INGREDIENTS

2 cups mashed potatoes

1 cup water (saved from boiling the potatoes)

4½ teaspoons active dry yeast

3 tablespoons sugar

1½ cups buttermilk or sour milk (see page 40), room temperature

6 tablespoons unsalted butter, melted and cooled

3 teaspoons salt

2 to 3 teaspoons dried crushed rosemary

5½ to 6½ cups Gluten-Free Flour Mix I (see page 198)

1 teaspoon xanthan gum

1. In a large bowl, mix the potatoes, water, yeast, and sugar; set aside until mixture begins to foam, about 5 minutes.

2. Pour buttermilk into the bowl of a stand mixer, fitted with paddle attachment. Add butter, salt, and rosemary and set mixer on low speed. Add 5½ cups flour mix, a little at a time, mixing until dough starts to get sticky. Turn mixer to high and mix for 4 minutes. (If making by hand, just work the dough with your hands until it's combined, about 8 or 9 minutes.)

3. Turn the dough onto a GF-floured work surface. Roll the dough out to ¾ inch thick, using a GF-floured rolling pin. With a serrated knife, cut dough into 2-inch squares. Place squares 1 inch apart on baking sheets lined with parchment paper. Allow rolls to rise for 15 to 30 minutes, covered with a damp tea towel.

4. Meanwhile, preheat oven to 375°F.

5. Bake for 18 to 20 minutes, until golden brown. Serve immediately.

GLUTEN-FREE CINNAMON ROLLS WITH CREAM CHEESE ICING

Unlike wheat-based risen breads, these GF cinnamon rolls do not require a lengthy rise time. They can be made in the morning when you want to serve them. The cream cheese icing is delicious and irresistible. **Yields 8 pieces**

INGREDIENTS

½ cup (1 stick) plus 2 tablespoons unsalted butter, divided

¼ cup granulated sugar

⅔ cup plus 3 tablespoons milk, divided

1 tablespoon active dry yeast

1 egg

¼ cup lard or virgin coconut oil, melted

1½ cups Gluten-Free Flour Mix II (see page 199)

¼ teaspoon xanthan gum

2 teaspoons baking powder

½ teaspoon salt

1 teaspoon maple extract

1 cup firmly packed brown sugar

1¼ teaspoons ground cinnamon

¼ cup whole cream cheese (not light or fat-free), room temperature

1½ cups powdered sugar

1. Preheat oven to 375°F. Generously grease a standard pie pan with butter; set aside.

2. In the bowl of a stand mixer, combine 2 tablespoons butter with sugar, and mix well.

3. In a small bowl, place ⅔ cup milk. Microwave for 30 to 60 seconds, until warm but not hot. Add yeast and stir until yeast is dissolved. Stir by hand into butter and sugar mixture.

4. Attach dough hook to mixer. Add egg, lard or oil, flour mix, xanthan gum, baking powder, salt, and maple extract, and mix until light and fluffy.

5. Place the dough between two sheets of plastic wrap that have been sprinkled with a little additional sugar to keep the dough from sticking, and flatten with your hand slightly. With a rolling pin, roll out to a 13- or 14-inch square. Let rest while you make the filling.

6. To make the filling, melt the remaining stick of butter in a microwave-safe bowl. Add brown sugar and cinnamon, and mix to combine.

7. Remove the top piece of plastic wrap from the dough. Spread the filling over the surface of the dough, clear to the edges. Roll up the dough, jellyroll-style. Cut off the ends, if desired for a neater edge, and cut the log into 8 equal slices. Place in the prepared pie tin and bake for 20 minutes, until tops are golden brown.

8. To make the icing, combine cream cheese, remaining 3 tablespoons milk, and powdered sugar in a small bowl. Using an electric mixer, blend until smooth.

9. Drizzle icing over the rolls as soon as they come out of the oven. Cool slightly before serving.

GLUTEN-FREE BANANA-BLUEBERRY BREAD

We love finding new ways to make classic breads gluten-free. If you have a bunch of overripe bananas lying around, make this with or without the blueberries. If you have perfectly ripe bananas, just peel and put in the microwave for a minute to release some of their sugar, and they will suffice in this recipe. **Yields 1 loaf**

INGREDIENTS

¼ cup virgin coconut oil or unsalted butter, melted

2 large eggs

¼ cup pure maple syrup

3 mashed bananas

2 teaspoons vanilla extract

¼ cup coconut flour

1 cup gluten-free oat flour

2 teaspoons baking powder

½ teaspoon salt

1 teaspoon ground nutmeg

2 tablespoons ground flaxseeds

1 cup frozen or fresh blueberries

1. Preheat oven to 350°F.

2. Grease a 9 x 5-inch loaf pan; set aside.

3. In a large bowl, whisk together the ¼ cup melted oil or butter, eggs, maple syrup, bananas, and vanilla until thoroughly combined.

4. In a separate bowl, mix the flours, baking powder, salt, nutmeg, and ground flaxseeds by stirring with a fork.

5. Combine the two mixtures and stir with a spatula or wooden spoon until thoroughly combined. Fold in the blueberries. Pour batter into prepared pan.

6. Bake for 50 minutes, until golden brown and a toothpick inserted in the center comes out clean. Cool for 5 minutes on a wire rack before turning out to cool completely.

GLUTEN-FREE SPICED PUMPKIN BREAD

Moist ingredients like pumpkin, applesauce, and other puréed fruits or vegetables are delightful when added to gluten-free recipes. They add moisture and help improve flavor and texture in this quick bread. **Yields 1 loaf**

INGREDIENTS

1½ cups puréed pumpkin (see page 84)

¾ cup sugar

½ cup virgin coconut oil, melted

2 large eggs

2 teaspoons vanilla extract

1¾ cups Gluten-Free Flour Mix I (see page 198)

2 teaspoons ground cinnamon

¼ teaspoon ground ginger

½ teaspoon salt

1. Place oven rack in the center of the oven. Preheat oven to 350°F. Grease a 9 x 5-inch loaf pan with coconut oil and dust with rice flour; set aside.

2. In a large bowl, combine pumpkin, sugar, oil, eggs, and vanilla. Beat with an electric mixer on low speed until mixed, about 1 minute. Set aside.

3. In a small bowl, stir together the flour mix, cinnamon, ginger, and salt. Add to the pumpkin mixture and beat on low until dry ingredients are just combined, about 1 minute. The batter will be thick.

4. Spoon batter into the prepared pan and bake for 45 to 55 minutes, until a toothpick inserted in the center comes out clean. Let the bread cool in the pan on a wire rack for 5 minutes. Run a knife around the edges of the pan to loosen the bread before turning it out to cool for an additional hour before slicing and serving.

GLUTEN-FREE CRANBERRY BREAD

This bread is so good with its mélange of holiday flavors that no one would guess it's gluten-free. Take it to your next potluck or office party, and watch it get gobbled up by GF and non-GF eaters alike. **Yields 1 loaf**

INGREDIENTS

2 cups Gluten-Free Flour Mix I (see page 198)

¾ cup granulated sugar

½ teaspoon salt

½ teaspoon baking soda

1½ teaspoons baking powder

1 teaspoon xanthan gum

½ teaspoon ground cinnamon

¼ teaspoon ground allspice

1 to 2 tablespoons orange zest

¾ cup freshly squeezed orange juice

¼ cup unsalted butter, melted

2 eggs

1 teaspoon vanilla extract

1 cup whole cranberries, fresh or frozen

1 cup chopped walnuts, divided

Sanding sugar, for sprinkling

1. Preheat oven to 350°F. Grease a 9 x 5-inch loaf pan with butter; set aside.

2. In a large bowl, sift together the flour mix, sugar, salt, baking soda, baking powder, xanthan gum, cinnamon, and allspice; blend with a whisk to combine. Set aside.

3. In another bowl, combine orange zest and juice, butter, eggs, and vanilla. Add to the dry ingredients and mix until just combined. Fold in cranberries and ¾ cup walnuts.

4. Pour batter into the prepared pan. Sprinkle sanding sugar and remaining ¼ cup walnuts over the top.

5. Bake for 45 to 55 minutes, until a toothpick inserted in the center comes out clean. Cool in the pan for 10 minutes, then turn out onto a wire rack and cool completely.

GLUTEN-FREE BANANA-NUT BREAD

Not only is there hardly any flour in this recipe, it's completely grain-free and dairy-free—with bananas, eggs, and nuts making up the bulk of ingredients. This banana bread is quite moist and flavorful and healthy, containing no refined sugar. **Yields 1 loaf**

INGREDIENTS

1½ cups mashed banana (about 3)

4 eggs

3 tablespoons honey

1 tablespoon vanilla extract

¾ teaspoon baking soda

½ teaspoon salt

1 teaspoon ground cinnamon

2 tablespoons ground flaxseeds

¼ cup plus 2 tablespoons coconut flour, divided

½ cup chopped walnuts (optional)

1. Preheat oven to 350°F. Generously grease a 9 x 5-inch loaf pan with butter or coconut oil; set aside.

2. In a large bowl, combine mashed bananas, eggs, honey, and vanilla; blend thoroughly. Add baking soda, salt, cinnamon, flaxseeds, and flour and blend until well combined. Fold in nuts, if desired. Set aside to rest for about 7 minutes.

3. Pour batter into the prepared pan and bake for 50 minutes, until a toothpick inserted near the center comes out clean. Cool completely in the pan on a wire rack before turning out and slicing.

GLUTEN-FREE PEANUT BUTTER BREAD

Peanut butter bread dotted with chocolate chips is a real kid- and crowd-pleaser. Most of this bread's sweetness comes from the small amount of stevia, though sugar is there as well for its texture and browning properties.
Yields 1 loaf

INGREDIENTS

2 cups Gluten-Free Flour Mix I (see page 198)

⅓ cup sugar

⅛ teaspoon pure stevia extract

1 tablespoon baking powder

1 teaspoon salt

1 teaspoon ground cinnamon

½ cup creamy peanut butter

2 tablespoons applesauce

2 teaspoons vanilla extract

1½ cups milk

½ cup chocolate chips

1. Preheat oven to 375°F. Grease a 9 x 5-inch loaf pan with butter or coconut oil; set aside.

2. In a large bowl, combine flour mix, sugar, stevia extract, baking powder, salt, and cinnamon; whisk to blend.

3. In another bowl, combine peanut butter, applesauce, vanilla extract, and milk; blend well. Add to dry ingredients and mix thoroughly. Stir in chocolate chips.

4. Pour batter into the prepared pan and bake for 40 to 45 minutes, until a toothpick inserted in the center comes out clean. Cool in the pan on a wire rack for 15 minutes. Remove from pan and slice as desired.

GLUTEN-FREE BUCKWHEAT BREAD

This recipe is not only gluten-free but it's grain-free as well. Buckwheat is not a grain at all but a fruit seed related to rhubarb and sorrel, making it suitable for people who are sensitive to wheat or other grains that contain protein glutens. All the grated and mashed vegetables in this recipe result in a supermoist, nutritious loaf. This recipe can also be made into 12 standard muffins; bake for 20 to 30 minutes. **Yields 1 loaf**

INGREDIENTS

1 cup almond flour

1 cup buckwheat flour

2 teaspoons baking powder

2 teaspoons ground cinnamon

1 tablespoon chia seeds

1 cup chopped walnuts

2 carrots, grated

2 zucchini, grated

1 cup mashed cooked sweet potato or pumpkin

2 eggs, lightly beaten, or 2 tablespoons tahini or applesauce

¼ cup virgin coconut oil, melted

1. Preheat oven to 350°F. Grease a 9 x 5-inch loaf pan with coconut oil; set aside.

2. In a large bowl, mix the almond flour, buckwheat flour, baking powder, cinnamon, chia seeds, and walnuts until well combined.

3. In another bowl, combine carrots, zucchini, sweet potato or pumpkin, eggs (or tahini or applesauce), and coconut oil; mix well. Pour into the dry ingredients and mix until well combined.

4. Pour the batter into the prepared pan and bake for 45 to 60 minutes, until a toothpick inserted in the center comes out clean.

5. Cool in the pan on a wire rack for 10 minutes before turning out to cool completely.

GLUTEN-FREE BLUEBERRY MUFFINS

These GF muffins are the closest thing you will get to "regular" blueberry muffins. With sugar, milk, eggs, and butter, the only difference is the gluten-free flour. **Yields 12 muffins**

INGREDIENTS

2 cups Gluten-Free Flour Mix III (page 199)

1 cup sugar

4 teaspoons baking powder

½ teaspoon salt

¼ teaspoon ground nutmeg

2 cups blueberries, fresh or frozen

2 eggs

⅔ cup milk

¼ cup unsalted butter, melted

TOPPING

¼ cup gluten-free flour

4 teaspoons sugar

2 tablespoons unsalted butter, chilled

1. Preheat oven to 350°F. Grease a standard muffin pan or line with paper cups; set aside.

2. In a large bowl, whisk together the flour, sugar, baking powder, salt, and nutmeg.

3. In a small bowl, combine all topping ingredients, then cut in the butter until mixture resembles coarse meal.

4. In a separate bowl, mix blueberries with ¼ cup of the topping mixture.

5. In a small bowl, beat the eggs; whisk in the milk. Add to the dry ingredients, then stir in melted butter. Fold in the blueberries. Divide batter evenly among 12 muffin cups and sprinkle the topping evenly over the batter.

6. Bake muffins for 20 to 25 minutes, until the tops are light brown and a toothpick inserted in the center comes out clean. Cool for 5 minutes in the pan on a wire rack before turning out to cool completely.

GLUTEN-FREE PIZZA CRUST

If you eat gluten-free, chances are you've missed pizza for a very long time. For some reason, GF pizza crust is quite an elusive thing, with most being too dry or too chewy, and all being virtually tasteless. This version calls for tasty sorghum flour and a good amount of spices and salt to bump up the flavor quotient. Say hello to pizza night again. **Yields 1 large crust**

INGREDIENTS

¾ cup warm milk (110°F) or water

1 tablespoon active dry yeast

2 teaspoons sugar

½ cup sorghum flour

½ cup tapioca flour

2 teaspoons xanthan gum

½ teaspoon salt

1 teaspoon Italian herb seasoning

2 teaspoons apple-cider vinegar

3 teaspoons olive oil, divided

White rice flour, for sprinkling

1. In a small bowl, combine milk, yeast, and sugar. In a large bowl, combine flours, xanthan gum, salt, and seasoning. Add yeast mixture, vinegar, and 1 teaspoon oil, and beat on low speed until blended, about 30 seconds. Dough will be soft.

2. Grease a 12-inch pizza pan generously with oil or lard. Turn dough onto the prepared pan and sprinkle with white rice flour. Press dough to the edges of the pan, continuing to sprinkle with flour to prevent sticking to your hands; make the edges thicker to contain toppings.

3. To bake: Preheat oven to 425°F. Bake topped pizza for 15 to 20 minutes until crust is golden brown and cheese is bubbling.

GLUTEN-FREE FOCACCIA

Flatbread, like this focaccia, is easy to make gluten-free. Mix up the dough, place it in a pan, let it rise, and press it out with your fingers. Top with tomatoes and garlic, or just infuse flavor into the dough with fresh or dried herbs—your choice. Always serve with a small bowl of extra virgin olive oil for dipping the finished focaccia.

Yields 6 servings

INGREDIENTS

¾ cup warm water (110°F)

1 teaspoon sugar or honey

2 eggs

2 tablespoons olive oil

½ teaspoon apple-cider vinegar

1½ teaspoons dry yeast

1 cup brown rice flour or garbanzo fava bean flour

½ cup tapioca flour

1 teaspoon unflavored gelatin powder

1½ teaspoons xanthan gum

1 teaspoon dried rosemary

½ teaspoon onion powder

¾ teaspoon salt

1. Combine warm water, sugar (or honey), eggs, oil, and vinegar in a large bowl. Using an electric mixer, beat on medium speed until very smooth. Add yeast, flours, gelatin powder, xanthan gum, rosemary, onion powder, and salt. Beat for 2 minutes. The dough will be soft and sticky, like thick cake batter.

2. Transfer dough to a greased 11 x 7-inch nonstick pan; or a greased 8-inch round nonstick pan; or a greased 15 x 10-inch nonstick pan. Cover with aluminum foil and let rise in a warm place for 30 minutes.

3. Preheat oven to 400°F.

4. Press dough out to flatten and sprinkle with additional seasoning, salt, and olive oil. If desired, top with a few cherry tomatoes and slices of garlic.

5. Bake for 15 minutes, until golden brown. If desired, drizzle additional olive oil on baked focaccia.

GLUTEN-FREE NAAN

This GF naan will knock your socks off, but only if you go to the trouble of toasting your quinoa flour. Toasting makes it slightly sweet and finer, with the consistency closer to an all-purpose flour. Toasted quinoa flour will also absorb moisture better when baking and will create more consistent results. It's quite easy and you can use the finished flour in all kinds of GF baking recipes.

Here's how to do it: Buy either organic, whole quinoa (recommended if you have a Vitamix or high-powered food processor) or organic quinoa flour. If using whole quinoa, grind it until flour forms. To toast, preheat oven to 220°F. Put the freshly ground or store-bought quinoa flour in a rimmed baking pan, no deeper than ¼ inch. Bake for 2½ to 3 hours. Remove from the oven and cool completely. Store flour in an air-tight container in the freezer for up to 6 months. **Yields 12 pieces**

INGREDIENTS

¾ cup warm water

2 teaspoons honey

2 teaspoons active dry yeast

1½ cups toasted quinoa flour

½ cup millet flour

½ cup potato starch

¼ heaping teaspoon xanthan gum

1 teaspoon fine sea salt

1 teaspoon garlic powder

½ cup cooked quinoa

1 tablespoon olive oil

1. In a small bowl, mix water with honey. Stir in the yeast. Set aside for 5 to 7 minutes, until foamy.

2. In the bowl of a food processor, combine the flours, potato starch, xanthan gum, salt, garlic powder, and cooked quinoa; pulse a few times to combine. Add the yeast mixture and oil, and process until dough begins to form.

3. With a greased measuring cup, scoop out ¼ cup of dough and shape into an oval flatbread about ¼ inch thick; place on a parchment-lined baking sheet. Repeat with remaining dough.

4. Cover flatbreads with a lint-free cotton or linen tea towel (terry cloth will stick and leave lint on the dough) and let rise in a warm place for 30 to 40 minutes, until puffy.

5. Place a few drops of olive oil in a 10-inch cast-iron skillet over medium-high heat. When hot, add naan, one at a time, and cook until golden on each side, flipping once, about 2 minutes per side, adding additional oil with each piece. Place on a sheet of foil and seal foil to keep them warm while cooking the remaining naan. Serve immediately.

GLUTEN-FREE BAGELS

The technique for GF boiled breads, like these bagels, is very similar to traditionally made ones; the ingredients differ only slightly. Customize this gluten-free recipe by adding raisins or cheese, ¼ teaspoon cinnamon, or ½ teaspoon dried onion flakes to the mixture. Or try sprinkling on sesame seeds or cinnamon sugar after boiling but before baking. **Yields 8 pieces**

INGREDIENTS

2 ⅓ cups Gluten-Free Flour Mix I (see page 198)

3 tablespoons nonfat dry milk powder

½ teaspoon salt

1½ tablespoons plus 2 teaspoons sugar, divided

2¼ teaspoons instant yeast

2 tablespoons unsalted butter, melted and cooled

1 egg, room temperature

3 egg whites, room temperature, divided

½ cup warm water plus 1 teaspoon water, divided

1. Preheat oven to 200°F. When the oven reaches temperature, turn it off.

2. In a large bowl, combine the flour mix, milk powder, salt, 1½ tablespoons sugar, and yeast. With an electric mixer on low speed, blend the ingredients. Add the butter, egg, and 2 egg whites to the dry mixture. Whip on low speed until blended. Add the ½ cup water and beat for 3½ minutes.

3. Turn dough onto a GF-floured work surface. Divide into 8 balls. Stretch out the ball and, with a GF-floured finger, punch a hole in the center.

4. Lightly grease a baking sheet with olive oil. Place each bagel on the baking sheet. Cover the bagels with lightly greased wax paper.

5. Set the baking sheet in the oven for 40 minutes to allow the dough to rise; it will not double in size.

6. Remove the baking sheet from the oven and preheat oven to 400°F.

7. Fill a large kettle with water (about 4 inches deep) and add the remaining 2 teaspoons of sugar. Bring the water to a boil.

8. Place 4 bagels at a time in the boiling water and boil for 1 minute, turning each bagel over after 30 seconds.

9. Cover the baking sheet with parchment paper. Remove the bagels from the water with a slotted spoon and lay them on the paper.

10. In a small bowl, whip the remaining egg white with 1 teaspoon of water until frothy. Brush the mixture on top of the bagels.

11. Bake the bagels for 20 minutes, until golden brown.

GLUTEN-FREE SOFT PRETZELS

Soft pretzels are a yeasty, delicious treat, best eaten straight out of the oven with yellow, Dijon, or grainy mustard. And you thought they couldn't be made gluten-free? Of course they can! **Yields 6 pieces**

INGREDIENTS

⅓ cup warm water

2¼ teaspoons active dry yeast

1 teaspoon sugar

1⅓ cups plus 2 tablespoons Gluten-Free Flour Mix I (see page 198)

½ teaspoon salt

1 egg

1 tablespoon honey or agave nectar

Olive oil, for brushing

⅔ cup baking soda, for water bath

1 tablespoon butter, melted, for brushing

Kosher or coarse sea salt

1. In a large bowl, whisk together the warm water, yeast, and sugar and let stand for 5 minutes. In a separate bowl, whisk together the flour mix and salt; set aside.

2. Add half of the flour mixture to the yeast mixture; add the egg and honey or agave nectar. With an electric mixer, beat on low speed for 1 minute. Add in the remaining dry ingredients and blend until well mixed. Form the dough into a ball with your hands. If the dough is too dry, add another teaspoon of water.

3. Divide the dough into 6 equal portions. Gently roll the dough pieces to about ¾ inch thick and twist each piece into a pretzel shape by placing the arc of the pretzel at the bottom (closest to you). Round the two ends so they're facing the arc and twist them around each other once. "Paste" them to opposite sides of the arc, using a little water, if necessary.

4. Place the pretzels on a baking sheet lined with parchment paper. Brush the pretzels generously with olive oil. Cover with a damp cloth and let stand in a warm place for 30 minutes.

5. Preheat oven to 375°F. Put 10 cups of water and the baking soda in a pot to boil. Stir well to dissolve the soda.

6. Once the soda bath is at a rolling boil, use a slotted spatula to carefully submerge pretzels, one at a time, into the water for 25 seconds, flipping over after 15 seconds. Do not boil longer or the pretzels may fall apart. Drain on a wire rack and replace onto the parchment-lined baking sheet.

7. Brush the pretzels with melted butter and sprinkle with salt. Bake for 12 to 15 minutes until light golden brown.

GLUTEN-FREE GLAZED BUTTERMILK DOUGHNUTS

If you've been wondering how to make gluten-free fried doughnuts, it's the same as making gluten-filled ones except you use a GF flour mix. We recommend using the Gluten-Free Flour Mix I on page 198 for this recipe.
Yields 1 dozen doughnuts and 1 dozen holes

INGREDIENTS

1½ cups Gluten-Free Flour Mix I (see page 198)

½ teaspoon baking powder

½ teaspoon baking soda

¼ teaspoon salt

¼ teaspoon ground cinnamon

¼ teaspoon ground nutmeg

2 tablespoons unsalted butter, melted and cooled

½ cup granulated sugar

1 egg, room temperature

½ cup buttermilk or sour milk (see page 40)

Lard or oil for deep frying

GLAZE

2 tablespoons butter, melted

1 tablespoon pure maple syrup

½ cup powdered sugar

1. In a large bowl, sift together the flour mix, baking powder, baking soda, salt, cinnamon, and nutmeg; set aside.

2. In the bowl of a stand mixer with the paddle attachment, mix the butter and sugar on medium-low speed. Add the egg and mix until smooth and creamy. Slowly pour in the buttermilk and continue mixing for 1 minute. Stop the mixer and add the flour mixture all at once. Mix on low speed, slowly increasing to medium speed and mix until well combined. Transfer the dough to a large bowl and cover with plastic wrap or a lint-free cotton or linen tea towel (terry cloth will stick and leave lint on the dough); refrigerate for 2 hours.

3. Heat 2 inches of lard or oil in a large kettle to 370°F.

4. Remove the dough from the refrigerator and turn onto a lightly GF-floured work surface. Dust the dough with GF flour and pat it out to ½ inch thick. Cut with a GF-floured 2½-inch doughnut cutter; separate the rings and holes.

5. With GF-floured hands, roll the doughnut holes into balls. Fry in the hot lard or oil until golden brown, about 2 minutes. Remove from fat with a slotted spoon and drain on a paper-towel-lined plate.

6. With a slotted metal spatula, drop doughnuts into hot fat, 3 at a time, and fry for 2 minutes, turning once, until golden brown. Remove with a slotted spoon and drain on a paper-towel-lined plate.

7. In a small bowl, whisk together the glaze ingredients until smooth. Drizzle on the cooled doughnuts and allow to set before serving.

METRIC CONVERSIONS

Please note that all conversions are approximate.

WEIGHT CONVERSIONS

U.S./U.K.	Metric
½ oz	14 g
1 oz	28 g
1½ oz	43 g
2 oz	57 g
2½ oz	71 g
3 oz	85 g
3½ oz	100 g
4 oz	113 g
5 oz	142 g
6 oz	170 g
7 oz	200 g
8 oz	227 g
9 oz	255 g
10 oz	284 g
11 oz	312 g
12 oz	340 g
13 oz	368 g
14 oz	400 g
15 oz	425 g
1 lb	454 g

OVEN TEMPERATURE CONVERSIONS

°F	Gas Mark	°C
250	½	120
275	1	140
300	2	150
325	3	165
350	4	180
375	5	190
400	6	200
425	7	220
450	8	230
475	9	240
500	10	260
550	Broil	290

LIQUID CONVERSIONS

U.S.	Metric
1 tsp	5 ml
1 tbs	15 ml
2 tbs	30 ml
3 tbs	45 ml
¼ cup	60 ml
⅓ cup	75 ml
⅓ cup + 1 tbs	90 ml
⅓ cup + 2 tbs	100 ml
½ cup	120 ml
⅔ cup	150 ml
¾ cup	180 ml
¾ cup + 2 tbs	200 ml
1 cup	240 ml
1 cup + 2 tbs	275 ml
1¼ cups	300 ml
1⅓ cups	325 ml
1½ cups	350 ml
1⅔ cups	375 ml
1¾ cups	400 ml
1¾ cups + 2 tbs	450 ml
2 cups (1 pint)	475 ml
2½ cups	600 ml
3 cups	720 ml
4 cups (1 quart)	945 ml
(1,000 ml is 1 liter)	

INDEX

ABOUT THE CREATORS

Karen K. Will is an enthusiastic bread baker, having run her own home-based artisan bread business, The Local Loaf, in Kansas. She is co-author, with her husband Oscar H. Will III, of *Plowing with Pigs and Other Creative, Low-Budget Homesteading Solutions* (2013).

The most popular and longest-running sustainable-lifestyle magazine, **Mother Earth News** provides wide-ranging, expert editorial coverage of organic foods, country living, green transportation, renewable energy, natural health, and green building. Lively, insightful, and on the cutting edge, *Mother Earth News* is the definitive read for the growing number of Americans who choose wisely and live well. Find out more at www.MotherEarthNews.com.

PHOTO CREDITS

Roger Doiron: 123

Lori Dunn: 91

Tammy Kimbler: 56

Jim Mackenzie: 13

Barbara Pleasant: 96

Karen K. Will: 21, 35, 37, 38, 39, 42, 51, 52, 77, 83, 99, 100, 101, 102, 146, 149, 151, 166, 169, 217

iStock: claudiad: 9 (bottom left); matejphoto: 9 (bottom right); Agorohov: 9 (center right); watcha: 9 (top left); meodif: 9 (top right); rudisill: 17; kcline: 18; NightAndDayImages: 23; JackJelly: 26; TheCrimsonMonkey: 29; JamesLoftus: 54; robynmac: 59; lamthatiam: 67; zingtime: 79; ginauf: 85; bhofack2: 87, 108, 111; Manu_Bahuguna: 95; violleta: 105; JB325: 106; MentalArt: 112; Anna_Kurz: 128; grandriver: 135; AntiGerasim: 136; ClimbOne: 138; AbbieImages: 159; EPerceptions: 173; Sohadiszno: 181; Yulia_Davidovich: 182; 58shadows: 183; jygallery: 185; sb-borg: 187; monkeybusinessimages: 189; sf_foodphoto: 192; marekuliasz: 197; ejwhite: 198; rozmarina: 201; jeangill: 202; MargoeEdwards: 209; emesilva: 213; Anna_Kurz: 215

Fotolia: Steven Miller: 69; dolphy_tv: 70; manyakotic: 73; jjava: 75, 140, 144; Joe Gough: 78; Stephanie Frey: 118; ckimballphoto: 124; NowPhotos: 126; fahrwasser: 130; daffodilred: 131; cook_inspire: 152; cobraphoto: 155; boyrcr420: 157; chas53: 170; Nadalina: 179; Andris T.: 204; maryskin: 211

Shutterstock: Magic cinema: 4; Vladislav Noseek: 6; Shawn Hempel: 7; LightField Studios: 10; vm2002: 25; Sunvic: 30; July Prokopiv: 32; ShotnCut: 46; chaechaebyv: 60; Ekaterina Smirnova: 65; Gordon Bell: 66; gowithstock: 80; Anna Shepulova: 92; Galiyah Assan: 116; Toasted Pictures: 121; Stephanie Frey: 142; Ozgur Coskun: 160; Karen Culp: 163; nelea33: 176; Katarzyna Wojtasik: 194